# Corporate Literacy

# CHANDOS
## KNOWLEDGE MANAGEMENT SERIES

Series Editor: Melinda Taylor
(email: melinda.taylor@chandospublishing.com)

Chandos' new series of books are aimed at all those individuals interested in knowledge management. They have been specially commissioned to provide the reader with an authoritative view of current thinking. If you would like a full listing of current and forthcoming titles, please visit our web site **www.chandospublishing.com** or contact Hannah Grace-Williams on email info@chandospublishing.com or telephone number +44 (0) 1865 884447.

**New authors:** we are always pleased to receive ideas for new titles; if you would like to write a book for Chandos, please contact Dr Glyn Jones on email gjones@chandospublishing.com or telephone number +44 (0) 1865 884447.

**Bulk orders:** some organisations buy a number of copies of our books. If you are interested in doing this, we would be pleased to discuss a discount. Please contact Hannah Grace-Williams on email info@chandospublishing.com or telephone number +44 (0) 1865 884447.

# Corporate Literacy

## *Discovering the senses of the organisation*

**A**NNE **K**AUHANEN-**S**IMANAINEN

**Chandos Publishing**
*Oxford • England*

Chandos Publishing (Oxford) Limited
Chandos House
5 & 6 Steadys Lane
Stanton Harcourt
Oxford OX29 5RL
UK
Tel: +44 (0)1865 884447 Fax: +44 (0)1865 884448
Email: info@chandospublishing.com
**www.chandospublishing.com**

First published in Great Britain in 2007

ISBN:
978 1 84334 261 8 (paperback)
978 1 84334 280 9 (hardback)
1 84334 261 8 (paperback)
1 84334 280 4 (hardback)

British Library Cataloguing-in-Publication Data.

A catalogue record for this book is available from the British Library.

Typeset by Replika Press, India.

Printed in the UK and USA

To Miska, Tanja and my Mother

# Contents

# List of figures and tables

## Figures

## Tables

# Acknowledgements

I want to thank Merja Karivalo for continuing support and inspiring discussions, during which the concept Corporate Literacy was formulated, Outi Peck, my sister, for translating the manuscript into English and as always for enlightening conversations and encouragement, Andrew Seymour and Lara Kauhanen for their thoughtful approach in editing the manuscript in English and Asko Simanainen, my husband, for his partnership in whatever I choose to pursue.

# About the author

**Anne Kauhanen-Simanainen,** MPolSc, has 20 years experience as an information designer, consultant and writer in the field of information and knowledge management and communications, before that she worked as a researcher in regional planning. The author's company CIM Communication & Information Management is situated in Helsinki. The author has worked for the Finnish government, ministries, research institutions, public agencies, companies and universities. During the last few years she has been developing continuing education courses for information professionals at the Helsinki University of Technology, specially on Information Architecture and Content Production.

The author may be contacted at:

*E-mail: anne.kauhanen-simanainen@ciminfo.fi*

# Introduction

The basis of successful research depends greatly on appropriately set questions. Physicist John Wheeler, who developed the concept of The Black Hole, gave the field of physics a phrase Big Questions: BQ and then, later on, Really Big Questions: RBQ in relation to physics and the whole of existence. The world of Information and Knowledge Management – both small- and large-scale tasks – can also be outlined based on a few essential questions relating to the research. Behind almost all of the projects I have been engaged in have been three big questions:

- How can polymorphous information, data and knowledge be utilised to support the decision-making, operations, development and innovations in organisations and corporations?

- How can the essential factors be filtered from the abundance of information?

- How can complex phenomena be better understood via information and knowledge?

Behind the *how* questions, is the difficult 'Really Big Question': *What* knowledge is important to our organisation? If an answer cannot be found to this question, all the other questions will remain hanging in the air. Yet there is one more question above it: Why? What knowledge is important for us to be able to create the necessary preconditions to ensure a good life for our children, grandchildren and generations far into the future? I would like to believe that this creation of preconditions that might ensure a secure life for future generations is the ultimate goal of all economic and social activities. While the world has 'shrunk', the chronological tension between present and future has become foreshortened. The 'Big Questions' concern our daily activities. Activities of both individuals and organisations may, in the networked, global world, have wider and more long-term consequences than perhaps ever before. The worrying aspect is that decisions and solutions may, in this fast and instantly reactive world, be based on incorrect information or ignorance. In this book I am exploring answers to the big questions within the field of information and knowledge through the application of the concept of Corporate Literacy.

This book has been written specifically for developers of organisations and corporate communities, information professionals and all who are interested in developing their organisations based on knowledge. The Corporate Literacy concept can be applied to companies, public administration and all corporations and communities involved in goal-oriented activities.

At the time of writing this introduction, information relating to several cartoons portraying the Prophet Muhammad published by a Danish newspaper has been spreading throughout the Muslim world. This has resulted in demonstrations and riots targeted at Danish embassies around the world. Information about the cartoons and the consequences of their publication is being transmitted around the world via TV, text messages and the Internet. The issue about what constitutes literacy relative to cultures, religions, social systems and media, based on which different corporate bodies select, evaluate and interpret the received messages is extremely topical.

## A new facet of information and Knowledge Management

Corporate Literacy is an aspect of corporate information culture and a new facet of Information and Knowledge Management. The approach it adopts is, however, quite different. Corporate Literacy involves critical but open and continuous information processing, whereas, administration and control are emphasised within the management approach. Companies try to gain control of information and knowledge using different methods with varying results. However, if management becomes the focus point, it will become detached from the actual functions it is designed for. In the worst case scenario it is possible to manage information efficiently even without actually utilising it. The core question is what information is important and how can it be fully utilised. Information and Knowledge Management establishes an information infrastructure but it is not the same thing as detection of information, reaction to it and its use in the decision-making process and operations. Developing comprehensive Corporate Literacy is essential for organisations in order to utilise the information resources organised and set up for use via management methods and technology.

## Focusing attention on information

What are the answers currently attributed to the big questions relating to information? On the social level, many states of the world, at the end of the twentieth century took as their goal the development of an information society with the intention of having broad-based access to Internet services, both as users and as content producers. The purpose of the states aiming to become information societies is the provision of Internet access to all of their citizens. In the ICT4 meeting organised in 2005, American IT expert Nicholas Negroponte and UN Secretary Kofi Annan, introduced a $100 laptop specifically designed for children in the countries of the developing world. The aim of the One Laptop per Child (OLPC) working group is to provide all the children of the developing world with these portable $100 computers, which can also be operated by cranking if there is no access to any external electricity source. This allows access to, even in the poorest circumstances, global information and the possibility of communication via the wireless network adapter built into the computers. The belief behind the project is that information may help in breaking loose from the cycle of hunger and poverty. The computer and the network connection are seen as key tools in terms of access to knowledge.

Information and communication technology, during the last decades, has been widely utilised by companies and public administration and its use has become a part of daily life in many parts of the world. This technology was first used in the management of numerical data information, then later on in the management of fact and reference information for full-text materials and finally in the management of visual and sound-based information. Almost all company information is already in a digital form. Various influential buzz terms have at different stages been used about methods and systems to manage information and knowledge: Information Resources Management, Document Management, Data Warehouse, Knowledge Management and Content Management. Libraries and information services have particularly aimed to provide information drawn from external organisations. The next big step to be taken both by companies and public administration is to integrate systems that were created at different stages and for different purposes so that the users do not have to learn to use each one separately. Instead, via a single interface, users can use an integrated system that both technically and semantically allows for reciprocal information flow between organisations' compatible systems.

Typical of all of these aims has been the paying of attention not just to technology, but also to the management of information and knowledge in certain *forms*, whether these include documents (Document Management, Information Resources Management, library and information services), data information (Data Warehouse), tacit knowledge, Knowledge Management or polymorphic non-structured content (Content Management). Information itself, the content, its meanings, stresses, source and quality have not been given that much attention compared with how much energy has been invested in the design and implementation of information systems. However, the information systems have not been able to produce the answers required. Users have still been faced with the problems and shortages of information. As almost all information is going to be managed digitally or electronically, it is high time attention was paid to information itself and the skills required of the organisation in using it.

## *Towards comprehensive literacy*

*The concept of Information Literacy* constitutes the answer to the question of how is it possible to filter, from the abundance of available information, the relevant information to the relevant areas. According to the American Library

Association, Information Literacy is a set of abilities requiring individuals to 'recognize when information is needed and have the ability to locate, evaluate and use effectively the needed information'. Information Literacy, particularly in scientific libraries, is taught to students from various academic disciplines as a part of higher education.

*Media Literacy* is very close to Information Literacy. Media Literacy means 'reading and writings skills' relating to different communication devices. Media Literacy is the ability to interpret mixtures of text, pictures and sound. A media literate person is able to distinguish relevant areas from the abundance of information and to use media by making independent choices. 'Writing skill' is the production and implementation of media, i.e. uses of text, pictures and sound in audiovisual media content. It is also essential to emphasise the usability of produced information, as we should not assume that people should only develop their information attainment and search skills as a response to increasingly more complex systems.

People working in large organisations often get lost in the jungle of numerous different systems. Efforts have been made to ease the operations of the individual. Usability research and user-oriented design look at information systems from the perspective of the user. The focus has been mainly on the individual, as according to Jacob Nielsen, the individual level has the most direct impact on screen design. Most websites, software applications and consumer devices are single-user designs. This level is also crucial since if individuals can't figure out how to work with your design, the larger levels become irrelevant. Group-level and enterprise usability demand a greater range of usability requirements. Jacob Nielsen states that individual usability is pretty much a solved problem, because there are good usability methods which can be learned and used by anybody. Group-level usability and enterprise usability are less well defined and need more research (Nielsen 2005).

## From Individual Literacy skills to Corporate Literacy skills

Information and Media Literacy skills together create continuity of literacy from evaluation of information needs to information production within a multimodular communication environment. *Digital and Network Literacy* represents the same continuity. These form the comprehensive literacy skills required for functioning within a networked information environment. These literacy skills, until now, have been considered from the perspective of the individual in much the same way as usability.

It is time when considering information and Media Literacy to focus on the corporate and organisation perspective. Views and conceptions relating to information, organisations and corporations need to be reassessed. What information is an organisation or corporation using? How is corporate information formed? What information is used in networked, polymorphic decision-making processes and operations? What kind of literacy skills are required by an organisation?

Over the years I have had the pleasure and the opportunity to collaborate on many projects and discuss numerous issues with Merja Karivalo, LicSc. Comprehensive *Corporate Literacy* (which was introduced for the first time in the earlier Finnish version of this book, see Kauhanen-Simanainen Anne and Karivalo 2002) became the major framework for our discussions. Our aim has been to build a synthesis of comprehensive literacy. Focusing on the concept of literacy in our discussions and writing has opened our eyes. Based on this concept both the organisation and information

7

seem even more complex and subtle, escaping simple definitions. The role of information and knowledge as an underlying basis for all human activity has gained even more importance.

## Surface and depth dimensions of information

The iceberg metaphor describes something fundamental within the current information environment and the use of information within that environment. In 2000 a company called Brightplanet, identified within the Internet a deep Web or an invisible Web. Search engines were unable to reach the documents contained within the deep Web. While search engines were able to access about one thousand million documents across the Web, the deep Web was a resting place for almost 550 thousand million documents. The quantity of documents, thereafter more than doubled within a few years. This finding was particularly interesting because the deep Web contains extremely high-quality information that is mostly free and is located in well-structured databases. It is being read by experts but is unknown to other Internet users. The current information and communication environment emphasises instant and easily accessible information. It is always possible to find something via Google and the media offers readily digested messages for worldwide attention 24 hours a day. 'The principle of least hassle' has long been established through research in human information behaviour. When this is considered in combination with the famous maxim by Professor Osmo A. Wiio: 'Communication is successful only by pure chance', it is obvious that the information grounds for decisions and operations are often shaky.

Literacy of organisations can easily remain just within the surface information. However, an iceberg may be drifting undetected beneath, creating the risk of a crash unless it is identified and understood. On a larger scale a conflict may be created between the activities visible on the surface and those taking place within the invisible layers deep below. This kind of conflict will create tension that will be discharged at some point. The discharges may appear as economic, political and environmental crises. Corporate Literacy means deep-level literacy, which aims to identify economic, cultural and environmental developmental processes. Along with fast-changing situation-related information, companies and organisations need slow-moving and deep-level formation of information and understanding for their strategic solutions and long-term future planning. One has to be aware of both levels.

Technology expands memory and information resources and furnishes new tools for information processing. By using modern technology it is possible to implement comprehensive integrated information systems which, via accurate searching, assist in the attainment of detailed information linked to time and place. Information can already be implemented on daily items, clothing and homes. Technology should no longer blind us with its miracles. Companies, public administration and citizens have to crystallise their goals, values and needs: it means making conscious choices on what information is important. We should also explore as to why at certain times, information is not reacted to, why it is not used as the basis for decisions, action instead, often being taken contrary to our better judgement?

## Discovering the sensory perceptions of an organisation

Sensory perception and intellect are the tools we use for processing what we observe, see and hear. As individuals we need to take good care of our brains and to keep our senses – our connectivity to the external-objective world – sharpened and alert to the complex environment and its information abundance – in the manner of our primeval ancestors with their heightened sensitivity to their natural environment where the need to be on one's guard was paramount. Or, as the captain of tanker carrying natural oil who had sailed the seas for 44 years said about sailing among the islands in the Baltic Sea said: 'We have to be as alert as if we were doing this for the first time' (Helsingin Sanomat 2005).

When working as corporate bodies and organisations we complement each others' skills and can achieve more than working alone. The creation of corporate literature means that even when we work as corporate bodies or organisations we discover our own sensory perceptions and use them in an active, rather than a passive manner. Working with information requires information and knowledge environments wherein information resources and flows are organised so that the intellect and individual sensory perception remain active and are allowed the space for vigilant observation, critical thinking and creativity.

The mutual relations between the individual, the organisation, information and work need to be re-evaluated leading to a shift in emphasis and attention in the following ways:

- from technology to knowledge;

- from information management to information itself: to observation, identification, selection, interpretation, application and utilisation of information;

- from individual Information Literacy to Corporate Literacy;

- from surface level to 'deep-level reading'.

The shifting of emphasis from individual skills to Corporate Literacy and the formation of knowledge is a real challenge particularly to the Western individual-oriented societies. Development of this kind of information culture is, however, essential in order for us to operate and solve our complex global and local problems. In order for us to utilise the sensory perceptions of the organisation, they first need to be discovered.

# 1

# Corporate Literacy:
# Why is it needed?

'When learning to read, the eyes open and it becomes possible to see oneself and the world in a new light'. This was once said by a Turkish woman, who had learnt to read as an adult. According to her 'being literate you are able to follow what happens, and you know your rights'.

Basic literacy is a necessary key to knowledge and to survival in modern society in all parts of the world. However, achievement of just basic literacy skills is nowadays insufficient, even in the least developed countries. The concept of Literacy is still expanding and it can be viewed from very different perspectives: Information Literacy, Media Literacy, Visual Literacy, Digital Literacy, Legal Literacy, Scientific Literacy Environmental Literacy, Global Literacy. However, the core and the basic meaning of comprehensive literacy is still the same: The eyes open and you see yourself and the world in a new light. Literacy is the skill we activate to 'read', observe, interpret, understand, evaluate and negotiate the context within which we operate.

Mostly, when discussing for example, Information or Media Literacy, the topic of discussion is the literacy of the individual person. A very broad-based literacy requirement is, however, an unrealistic goal for individuals, even for information professionals. The connection of an organisational perspective to literacy makes the goal achievable. Even though information and Media Literacy have been around for a long time and are a well documented subject, especially in an academic context, they have hardly been discussed in the corporate environment. When the concept of literacy is placed in the corporate context it becomes apparent that it is necessary to take into account the whole literacy spectrum and create a synthesis of it.

Corporate Literacy is a comprehensive set of skills and information flows activated by a company or an organisation for implementation of its strategic goals. Essentially the organisation is able, through the development of its Corporate Literacy, to gain a better understanding about the issues considered important than would otherwise be possible via the total sum of the information skills and knowledge of its individual members. Via its literacy the organisation observes, interprets and forms knowledge from its operational environment, its customers as well as from its own role, status, resources, possibilities and risks. Based on its literacy the organisation will analyse the current situation, take soundings about the future and reflect upon the historical perspective. Many companies and public sector organisations suffer from the problem of being self-centred and as a result, blind to the views and needs of the customers and citizens, while simultaneously ignorant of new operational possibilities and methods. Based on effective literacy an organisation can see the world and its own situation and opportunities in a new light.

# Accepting complexity and unpredictability

Globalisation, financial insecurity, political crises and environmental problems produce reverberations around the globe as well as in the operational and decision-making environment. The world has 'shrunk' and the links between issues, reasons and causation are complex, resulting in rapid and often surprising consequences. These consequences have knock-on effects for individuals, companies and states. The media, the Internet and mobile services offer continuous information, weighing down human consciousness and thought processes, making it difficult to tease out the essential issues.

Complexity and unpredictability are issues we can no longer ignore or avoid. 'We just got to go through it', like the children sing in the song 'I am hunting a lion-a-hunting', whether facing a swamp, a jungle or a scary cave. One has to go through whatever is in one's path, all the time remaining alert and ready to react.

I often wander around the Academic Bookshop in Helsinki, within its light, three-storey space, where it is possible to walk along undisturbed, to browse books and to lose oneself in them for hours and hours. Just like in all up-to-date bookshops, the literature displayed projects a current view of the world and its phenomena. Globalisation, climate change and terrorism, are extremely visible in the year 2006. Experts, parliaments, governments, companies planning their business operations, media houses and ordinary citizens wish to understand these wide-ranging phenomena. What has to be accepted and understood is their complexity in order to be able to construct literacy skills that can successfully embrace them. On this basis it might be possible to understand these phenomena better and to get ready to react to them in an appropriate manner.

## The first example: the global economy

Globalisation can be viewed from economic, societal, social and cultural perspectives. The market economy has spread to almost every part of the world. International competition between companies, economic booms, depressions and various fluctuations are reflected from one continent to another. Capital and workforce move accordingly to locations currently offering the most cost-effective operating conditions and, as a consequence, available employment. Information networks remain connected 24 hours a day, 7 days a week. This connective state is even maintained during national days of celebration and Bank holidays. The demands for continuous preparedness and availability and the accelerating work tempo test both individuals and companies. A decision by a company to move its business operations to another side of the globe may suddenly result in the redundancy of the whole workforce of a particular community, forcing the members of that community to rely exclusively on any welfare state benefits that might be available to them. Of course, it is often the case in poorer countries that no such benefits exist, meaning the newly redundant workforce and their dependants are deprived of any income whatsoever. In China in particular, and Asia as a whole, globalisation has enabled rapid economic development. Globalisation brings distant and strange phenomena into the daily lives of ordinary people or moves the basic fundamentals of daily living, such as a job and a home, to other parts of the world. Large rivers of immigration flow from one country to another. Currently 190 million people are working outside their own country. Cultures and religions meet or clash with each other in business, residential areas, at work and in human relationships. Globalisation is seen as both positive and negative. Ultimately, however it is viewed, it is a fact requiring companies and states to set their relationships and strategies according to its continuously changing demands.

Companies have to be able to 'read' globalisation from the perspective of their own operations: markets, potential locations, access to raw materials, available workforce and related costs. Literacy has to cover the needs of customers and personnel, effects of culture, surrounding social, economic and cultural circumstances and legislation affecting business operations. The establishment of networks requires profound literacy skills. When setting up joint ventures in another cultural environment on the other side of the world it is difficult to know who to trust and what are the true interests of the parties concerned. Companies spread their tentacles throughout networks, latching on to relevant bits of information about the surrounding community. Inappropriate use of networks may lead to difficulties and unintentional selection of the wrong party. It is incumbent upon companies to continuously re-evaluate and review their information channels.

The question to ask is what is happening below the visible surface and to search for information that is not instantly visible or available. Deep information flows and slow evolution processes move below instantly accessible information. In addition to listening to others when debating, it is also important to reach for the deeper meanings and processes that could lie beneath the verbal expressions. It is also important to ask what the future may bring. The greater the difference as regards the cultural and political background, history and circumstances, the more alertness is required in the pursuit of understanding.

Politicians and the leaders of the state as well as the citizens and their associations need to understand globalisation and its effects. 'There is a growing concern about the direction globalisation is currently taking', states the report issued by the World Commission on the Social Dimension of Globalisation, co-chaired by President Tarja Halonen of Finland and President Benjamin William Mkapa of Tanzania. 'Its advantages are too distant for too many, while its risks are all too real. Corruption is widespread. Open societies are threatened by global terrorism, while the future of open markets is increasingly open to question. Global governance is in crisis. We are at a critical juncture and we need to urgently rethink our current policies and institutions.' (International Labour Office 2004).

The Commission held 26 consultations in over 20 countries concerning globalisation. In the kaleidoscope of opinions they also found much common ground. This included a general sense of insecurity and concerns about employment.

Globalisation has been and is being interpreted by many different parties and there have been and continue to be numerous articles, books and reports written about it. An equitable rolling out of globalisation depends on better national and global governance. Empowering people to participate effectively in the opportunities of globalisation is extremely important. Information and communication are necessary tools for people, companies and communities. We all need to be able to be literate as regards globalisation in order to avoid becoming its unwilling victims.

## Second example: the earth's changing climate

It is typical of environmental problems that there is already plenty of information concerning a predicted future. However, people don't usually react to information prior to anything alarming taking place: thus waterways are already polluted and the quality of air has already deteriorated quite considerably. The concept of global warming has been known for a considerable time. The debate has mainly been concerned as to what degree is the warming a result of the actions by human beings. The International Panel on Climate Change (IPCC) has already published in 1990, a report warning about serious future consequences unless the decision-makers intervene in the matter. Based on the same international panel the only question now is how fast the change will take place. No one can reasonably claim that information is lacking concerning the risks to the environment as a consequence of human activities.

Literacy regarding environmental issues has been consistently relegated to a status of low priority during the twentieth century. Current ecological damage has already exceeded the tolerance threshold of the earth by 20%. The ongoing climate change affects all human beings and it needs a reaction at local, regional and state levels and requires international agreements. We need an extremely high-quality literacy level for us to be able to interpret the research results relating to climate change and to apply the information on our activities and daily life.

In the summer of 2005 the TV showed news relating to the destruction caused by hurricane Katrina in Louisiana, on the south-western coast of the USA. This natural disaster was one of the most destructive in US history. The force and strength of hurricanes and the consequent surges of the sea are expected to increase in line with what environmental experts have long been warning in all parts of the world. Even in the relatively calm climates of the Nordic countries urban areas have been hit by floods and there have been an increased number of extreme weather conditions in the last 10–20 years. What is most alarming is information identifying a thawing of the western Siberian permafrost. The fear is that it is an indication that a complete reversal of the greenhouse effect, and thus the consequences it produces, is no longer tenable. Climate change is a reality and the signs are visible in various locations. However, people tend to wake up to such issues only when the flood-waters are lapping at their front door.

Information relating to climate change is not accessed within the decision-making processes and operations of companies, states and cities with the seriousness that this global phenomenon requires and there have been efforts to manipulate the research data to suit specific interests. Climate change is a good example of an issue where the citizens, political decision-makers, companies and authorities require fluency in a scientific literacy in order to facilitate an accurate assessment of the situation at the frontline and thereby be in a position to make appropriate decisions regarding their own operations. A cross-section of information sources is required so that a comparison can be made across a range of results in the context of competing background interests, aims and goals. The relationship between the necessary caution displayed by researchers in drawing conclusions and the formation of a body of reliable scientific knowledge has to be understood. However, climate change is an issue everybody can have an effect upon via their conduct in carrying out daily activities. It is also clear that the global society as a whole is rapidly approaching the 11th hour in terms of preventing the worst predicted scenario as regards global warming.

Absolute certainty about the final outcome of climate change is likely to be available only when it is too late. The effects of climate change are both financial and political, which means that trading and commercial interests, not to mention politicians, are eager to consolidate information which appears to serve their own interests. When the results of science and research are being filtered via the media, they are also being filtered through many informational layers, which include the vested interests of the media, transformation sponsors of the research as well as the political goals of the government of the day. These layers and their effects should be identified in order to allow a more accurate interpretation of the information transmitted.

In the midst of future environmental crises we may need to rely on highly tuned anticipatory literacy and operational skills as our primeval forebears relied upon an acutely honed natural instinct. Paradoxically, we may, in the decades ahead, become increasingly dependent on nature and its phenomena in all parts of the world. This will have an effect upon the performance of companies, public administration and all of our personal lives. A wide array of literacy skills are required when deciding upon the best use of natural resources, the planning and construction of cities, holiday resorts and individual buildings.

Organisations, communities and societies, can be viewed as systems operating and taking guidance according to the prevailing currents of information and communication flows. These information and communication flows have an important role in the development and transformation of these systems. Donella Meadows, Jorgen Randers and Dennis Meadows write in their book, *Limits to Growth: The 30 year Update* (2004), that information is a key component in the move to sustainable development. It doesn't necessarily mean that we need more information, better statistics, larger or global databases, though they also have their part to play. What is needed is essential, immediate, selective, consolidated, current and accurate information. According to these system theorists all systems will start to behave differently when their information flows are changed. They also argue that systems strongly resist changes in their information flows as this leads to new regulations and goals.

Donella Meadows, Jorgen Randers and Dennis Meadows believe that it is still possible (being the only tenable choice) to move swiftly down the road to sustainable development. I think that it requires not simply information, but rather an active Corporate Literacy. The matter is too complex to be dealt with and understood individually. The decision-making process of the leading politicians, of companies and even of the leaders of states cannot be based on their personal knowledge and visions or even on those of the close circle of individuals around them. Decisions should be made and assessed using wide and versatile literacy. In respect of political decisions and decisions by authorities, the information that provides the grounds for those decisions should be transparent to all citizens.

The better an organisation can read and understand its operational and information environment, its multilayered information sources and multiplicity of information content, the better the chance it has to survive, to influence its own future, the future of others and ultimately, to succeed in a world of continuously changing circumstances. Corporate Literacy as regards climate change requires information, media, target specific information (in this case, environmental information) and scientific literacy on the part of companies, public administration and citizens' organisations. Organisations require monitoring systems producing accurate information, results of long-term research, signals communicating about changes, widespread assessment of the relationships of reasons, consequences and effects. Common to all these examples is the complexity, multiplicity, network basis and fragmentation of the phenomena and therefore the relationships of reasons and consequences are difficult to find but are manifested and have an effect locally to individual companies, organisations and people and their daily lives. We will form our views about all these based on the information we receive from a variety of communication channels and our own experience.

This is an environment and reality, which offers possibilities, but also, inevitably, sets restrictions. We have to sail along with the flow or against the flow depending on which direction we want to go at any given moment in time. Through the development of Corporate Literacy, companies and public administration will gain greater access to skills and resources, vital in managing ever-changing situations. The complexity and unpredictability of the environment will not appear so threatening, and instead, can be accepted as the norm.

In the drama called *Albert Speer* by David Edgar (2000) Hitler's favourite architect answers the accusations of Nazism levelled against him as follows: 'I didn't know. I could have known but I never asked questions'. Albert Speer was later promoted to Minister of Armaments and War Production and he was the second most powerful man in Nazi Germany. It seems that Speer lied to himself, as well as others, to be able to live with his conscience. Is future climate change the phenomenon we knew of, but never asked questions about? In order to stop this happening, we need Corporate Literacy, which requires all of us to ask questions and to search for answers.

## Third example: terrorism

Many current affairs books are dealing in the summer of 2005 with terrorism and the causes underlying it, about which the Western world is eager to find out. Why is this going on? Where does this hostility spring from? A whole army of writers are producing articles and books about terrorism; media interviewers are grilling experts in different fields and from different parts of the world; and discussions are active across the Internet, in cafes and on public transport. Confusing statements are being publicised; while new perspectives, greater background information and fresh interpretations are in constant demand. Millions of people: political decision-makers; stock brokers; travel agents; and security personnel all require a better understanding of both the reasons for, and the consequences of, terrorism. Terrorism can have an effect on anybody, either directly or indirectly via a complex network of connections. The experiences of the victims and their families are a heavy burden to carry. Terrorism has a significant effect on people's sense of security, their travel decisions, their monitoring of the environment, trade and commerce, indeed of society as a whole. In order that society can arrive at an appropriate and properly measured response to this phenomenon, the underlying causes and general background to terrorism need to be identified with greater clarity than exists at present.

The underlying causes and the general background appear complex. They include wars and poverty but this does not prevent individuals born in affluent countries with no personal experience of poverty from carrying out terrorist deeds. It also appears that the decision-makers and the majority of Western populations find it difficult to relate to the circumstances, feelings and aims, which result in large numbers of immigrants making their way to Western shores. There is a simultaneous effort to find out what the Islamic religion represents at its core. The media seeks out experts in the Islamic religion to provide them with interviews. It is very difficult to understand what actually lies at the core of any religion, not least because the parts played by religions and cultures in the flow of the events are so frequently misinterpreted.

Terrorism is an example of an issue that requires comprehensive literacy skills. It requires literacy skills for the understanding of history, religions, cultures and human situations. An approach based on comprehensive literacy is essentially different from the one based on narrowly focused understanding and swift situation assessment. Terrorism is an example of an issue where a company, national parliament and authorities, as well as citizens' organisations, should be able to obtain, sift and analyse information thoughtfully and broadly. What is needed is an ability to distinguish which information is important and an ability to sift through information sources representing different perspectives.

An organisation engaged in international operations requires information channels and senses and needs to pick up soundings from events in different parts of the world not to mention a method for the detection of important signals. 'Currently we all need to watch what is happening in different parts of the world', said a travel company manager after London's terrorist strikes. An organisation needs information about current events and it should also be able to formulate its own understanding about the underlying development processes and their consequences. Companies need to observe what the citizens, politicians and authorities think and do in order to be able to evaluate their own operations from this basis. Equally, the political decision-makers and authorities have to be aware about the operations of various bodies and the effect of events on these. Corporate Literacy means continuous critical assessment and renewal of the information channels and networks used and of one's own understanding in accordance with the changing situations. The leaders of the states also need to be able to evaluate critically each other's operations and reactions.

## Changing the concept of an organisation

Our idea about an organisation is changing along with the networking, information flows and globalisation. Many of the previous operational models and management methods are in conflict with the new kind of operational environment; neither can they respond to its requirements. Corporate Literacy as a concept supports the idea of an organisation as complex, self-organising operational patterns based on people's interaction, power, relationships and contracts. (This kind of an idea of an organisation is presented f. ex. in Stacey 2003.) The production and service range offered by companies and the public administration is the result of interactions between large numbers of people and corporations. No man is an island. Nor single corporation. Organisations have an effect on each other and their operations are based on, and interact across, a wide variety of networks. This kind of thinking leads to an entirely different vision of information flow. This new vision contrasts with the traditional vision that views information flow as being hierarchic, rigid, uniform and controlled and managed from above. In the new vision, people are seen as active network operators in a system where their participation and contributions are taken into account at all levels.

People do not belong to organisations as their subordinates. They only undertake to allocate their time, skills and contribution to various joint matters based on the terms set out in mutually agreed contracts. These contracts can be signed between the employee and the employer. In practice, these can have a judicial basis, can be based on culture, religion or some other tacit basis, in writing or by means of a verbal agreement alone. An organisation, in essence, is an expression of these joint activities and commitments. The better network activities are understood, the less valid becomes our current conceptualisation of what constitutes an organisation. Self-organisation and actions as communities of practice become more visible both from internal and external perspectives. This improved understanding will lead to change and development in current organisations and administrative structures. This new vision of information flows offers increased possibility for mutually beneficial economic and social activity and for people's personal actions and initiatives.

Within and between organisations, it is possible to form flexible and transformative communities targeted toward the solution and implementation of required tasks and needs. They can be created consciously to solve a specific problem or they can be created in a self-organising manner. Their lifespan is dependent upon the length of time the common aim is maintained and the type and terms of the mutual agreement. Based on their corporate knowledge and literacy they can deal with complex issues. Furthermore, they are sites of intense corporate learning. Information is linked in new ways in the corporations formed by people coming together from different fields. This provides the possibility of creating so called in-between innovations; new creative solutions that would not be possible by even the best expert or experts representing one field alone. (For more about various in-between organisations see Johansson 2004.) These kinds of innovations are created only when experts from different fields, representing, as they do, different concepts, cultures and knowledge, clash. Such a clash can result in a change of scientific direction, new products, services, and technologies, as well as new ways of functioning in modern daily life.

If one regards these kinds of communities as cells joined to one another, it then appears logical to ask what is the task or 'nucleus' of each of the cells bound together. It is the nucleus that sets the literacy requirements of the cell. Locating the nucleus can be a problem within an industrial process that needs to be solved through rapid information compilation via a virtual project, where the different project members are located in different parts of the world and represent different views as regards the problem. The 'nucleus' could be an elderly person, living at home and suffering from a long-term illness whose help and service requirements have to be planned and organised. One person is unlikely to be able to assess the whole picture complicated as it is, by the associated medical and social issues. An expert team with specialist knowledge relating to the situation and the needs of the elderly person is required. The team has to be formed from representatives of all the relevant fields who have the literacy skills to be able to deal both with the patient, and the multidimensional information required by the situation. The team has to be able to convert the different expertise represented by its members into a collective understanding. The elderly person is the nucleus whose needs and goals determine the information strategy.

Meadows *et al.* (2004) state in their book *Limits to Growth* that it is difficult to spread new information in a system that has been set to only listen to old information. The structural setting of information is affected even by the way the organisation or the community is formed. The cells described above are open to new information because of the flexibility of their information structure. Their information flows are based on task and customer-based needs, not on static organisational structures.

Corporate Literacy is reflected in the information architecture created by the corporation for itself. Information architecture is also a necessary requirement for continued development, the concrete structures via which information flows are filtered and selected. Information architecture is discussed later on in this book. Corporate Literacy analyses organisations and structures their information environments so that they are able to receive new information and to renew their information and communication flows.

The fundamental issue is still what constitutes the goals, contracts, power relationships, economic, judicial and political structures based on which the companies, public administration and various corporations operate. The complexities within the network operations and the models for global operations between regions, organisations and corporations are still opaque. For the construction of their own operational model, organisations and corporations need a comprehensive literacy with a clear strategy as its basis: why do they function and what kind of information is important to them? In the future, working environments will continue to be managed on the basis of financial criteria being strictly target-oriented. However, the markets, more than ever, will exhibit a need for flexibility and the ability to react rapidly.

## The communal and collaborative process

Even in Western individualistic societies, communality is sought after in various areas of life. Network communities are established, involving communal learning, working together, and a discussion of interactive processes. Continuous interaction and acquisition of information and progression of the collaborative process belong to the communal process. Literacy has to be based on the terms of the process. These operational methods cannot be adopted spontaneously. They can even be in conflict with the current operational patterns emphasising individual achievements and effectiveness and end targets of the industrial society.

Interdisciplinary and inter-vocational cooperation is increasingly needed. In the case of companies it may mean the combining of technical, marketing, sales and product development expertise. User-centred design is required for product development, meaning that customer or user groups have to be recognised as legitimate participating parties in the design process. The role of communal working has been recognised in science and culture. The myth about solitary researchers in their chambers is a thing of the past; research is undertaken in groups.

Process-based working is being explored both in engineering and artistic work. The role of processes and their support is emphasised in the network environment. For example, a website producer does not know what the end target of use for the website may be. Hypertext is not built into a story with a beginning and an end but the text continuously offers options and links for the readers based upon their own choices to move forward and to build their own processes. The same feature exists in e-learning.

Many of the leading theatres, ballet companies and orchestras want to emphasise the creative process as a team effort rather than an individual performance. Furthermore, in the visual arts the attention has moved on to an appreciation of the artistic process instead of a simple admiration of the final, completed result. This is shown in environmental works of art involving artefacts being structured in a natural environment or in art videos showing the fading of a plant or events in a particular urban situation. The process has no end nor has it any definable borders. A piece of art can be a building and a change within it or the artists could be working in interaction with some local community with the most important thing being the interactive process itself, rather than any individual piece of art created by it.

Organisational and Corporate Literacy has to be a built-in aspect of working processes. Corporate Literacy also requires communal thinking and information culture. The better working, knowledge and information processes are understood and the communal information culture supported, the better are the conditions for the development of Corporate Literacy.

## Changing the perception relating to information and knowledge

Information and knowledge have various definitions. There is no one, generally accepted definition, about knowledge and information. There exists, in practice, a fairly common and established view relating to the value chain from data to information, from information to knowledge, then further to wisdom and then further still to unity. This value chain is not, however, logically valid but can also be turned the other way around: wisdom is needed for the formation of knowledge, knowledge is needed for the collecting, processing and editing of information and information is needed to form data. Hans Christian von Baeyer (2004) poses information to be the Really Big Question of science. The definitions of humanistic information and of technical/natural scientific/mathematical information theories are far apart. The former being broad, while the latter group, being solely quantitative, are therefore too narrow. Baeyer hopes that these views will one day be combined.

In practice, different views can be combined, at least to some degree. Well aware of the complexity relating to the definitions of information and knowledge I will aim to use these concepts in the context of the following definitions.

## *Information*

By information I mean externalised knowledge and meanings. They may be conveyed with letters, numbers, photos, computer bits or sound, for example. Knowledge converted to information can be communicated, transferred and stored. Information can be seen, heard or touched. Information does not necessarily have any truth value. It can be shown to be right or wrong. It can be based on observation but also on belief. The quality and correctness of information can be evaluated. This view, as regards information, is a mixture of the mathematical information theory (information can be measured by changing the message content to bit codes) and humanistic view, including the semantic content (information carries meanings).

From the point of view of the user, information can be said to represent 'utility consumables'. It is searched for, sifted, collected, edited, published and transferred. Elizabeth Orna calls information the 'food of knowledge' because 'we need information and communication to nourish and maintain our knowledge and keep it in good shape for what we have to do in the world. Without the food of information, knowledge becomes enfeebled' (Orna 2004).

Knowledge is formed when an individual decodes the meaning of new information, connects it to her previous knowledge and thereby forms a relevant aggregate. The basis of knowledge is founded on things learned in the past, experiences, memories, observations, language and interaction between people and the external world. We have knowledge that we can formulate and so-called tacit knowledge that we cannot express specifically, but which is shown in our actions and behaviour. Formation of knowledge within organisations and corporations is created in a similar way.

## Knowledge

If no generally acceptable definition is found for 'information', it is even less likely to be found for 'knowledge'. The philosophical concept of knowledge emphasises the truth value of knowledge. We talk about semantic, pragmatic, operative and orientative knowledge. Knowledge Management thinking has combined tacit knowledge and expertise to form the Western knowledge concept.

If all the different definitions with their extensions were to be combined, we would be faced with a very broad and multidimensional issue. However, we have various definitions that are not continually defined in discourse. When dealing with knowledge, we create wisdom, evaluate our knowledge, talk about a knowledge society, etc. The issue being debated is helped when we tie it to a context and to the social and cultural situation and framework. However, this debate is not easy and at times we will find that we are talking about different topics using the same words. However, strict definitions with no in-depth basis will not assist the debate but, rather, restrict it and could make it entirely fruitless. Knowledge is not static, permanent, or limited; it is continually being recreated via shared evaluation of the social and cultural environment, knowledge distribution, processing, thinking and connecting.

Unwritten traditional knowledge and wisdom of indigenous peoples represents a comprehensive way in which to perceive the world. The sharing of knowledge and its communality are the central features. The view taken of knowledge in Western societies has also become more expansive. Nonaka and Takeuchi from Japan have created a theory of cyclic knowledge process, which takes into consideration both the expressed, explicit and tacit knowledge as well as their interaction. Networking of the information and communication systems consolidates the communal nature of knowledge and memory. In the web environment there are phenomena that augur well for the emergence of new kinds of possibilities for the formation of communal knowledge. These include an open source community, open access publishing wikipedia, and communal information classification practices called folksonomy. Weblogs on the other hand strengthen the visibility of individual information interpretation.

It is difficult to locate knowledge. Based on Knowledge Management theories it is thought that tacit knowledge is formed and then somehow stored inside the heads of individuals. As long as individuals and organisations have been perceived as separate entities, it has been thought that knowledge could be removed from the heads of individuals, externalised and then stored as so called explicit knowledge, which would then become a form of knowledge capital belonging to the organisation. However, from the perspective of the theory of complexity, knowledge is always formed through an interactive process and the ability to interact is an essential feature of knowledge. Knowledge cannot be located in the heads of individuals for distribution within an organisation. Knowledge is a result of a discourse and new knowledge is created when the ways to speak and interact change (Stacey 2001). Nor can knowledge be anymore located accurately and rigidly into a certain organisation such as a university or administrative authority. New knowledge is formed in large and small companies, local corporate bodies and among citizens. Nor is the reliability of knowledge closely connected to a certain organisation. Knowledge, just like the corporate bodies formed by people, is continually changing. Therefore, the evaluation of knowledge is difficult.

However, we can build processes where knowledge is obtained, analysed and processed in accordance with certain criteria, which can be checked, in much the same way as in scientific research. We can, and should, set quality requirements for knowledge. It is important that we are able to distinguish knowledge based on scientific research from subjective practical experience, from assumptions of knowledge based on observations, empirical knowledge from theoretical, etc. At the same time it is important to be aware that none of these information and knowledge types covers the entire knowledge concept. We need them all. Therefore, we also need skills for processing and connecting different knowledge types: a broad, yet critical and evaluative literacy.

## Communication as part of knowledge

Corporate Literacy is a communal, interactive process. Literacy changes and develops all the time in shared interaction. It is not the skill we once learnt, such as learning our ABC, but the way the developing skill receives, interprets, analyses, organises and produces new knowledge. An essential part of modern literacy is the skill to use various communication forms, equipment and channels and, prior to anything else, the skill to communicate and learn.

Knowledge and communication cannot be separated from each other. Knowledge by itself is a result of communication and effective utilisation of knowledge requires sharing. Not a single knowledge system should be designed without taking into consideration its communicative features, usability, intelligibility and the utilisation of knowledge. These can be designed only by knowing the users of the knowledge, their needs, knowledge habits and communication methods. The mutual connections between people, activities, information systems and communication have simultaneously to be taken into consideration. Knowledge is created as a result of interaction between people and the environment and the creation of new knowledge requires a transfer of knowledge on to one more grade further along the refinement process.

We increasingly work among demanding large-scale tasks and complex service entities where the typical feature is non-ending and interdisciplinary-based collaboration. Health care in industrialised countries is a good example. Increasing numbers of long-term illnesses, such as adult diabetes, often in tandem with other illnesses, not to mention increasingly lengthening average life spans, increases the need for health care services. Typically, many of these illnesses are manageable rather than curable. It is therefore, imperative, that health services should provide appropriate assistance for the whole life span of the individual.

The same non-ending and multidimensional basis relates to very different kind of phenomena such as comprehensive networked information systems and product development intended for global use. Integrated information systems with their network services and background systems are extremely complex entities, which should keep up with the changes in the operations of their provider, requirements of the users and juridical and technical reviews. Product development must allow for market changes, adjustment to the needs of customers, as well as the competitiveness of the company. All these require comprehensive Corporate Literacy and interpretation of all processes in their entirety. Based on the expertise of just one person or just one group representing one specialised field, these issues cannot be resolved, not even discussed.

## Sustainability and balance

Our primeval ancestors had a strongly developed primordial literacy as regards nature. It is a skill to manage to live as a part of nature. To survive together with nature in our current overpopulated world is a skill that individuals, companies and societies have to re-learn. The bad news is that we need to re-learn this long lost skill as quickly as possible. The limits for growth and expansion have already been exceeded in terms of planet Earth and we will have to struggle with the environmental changes created as a consequence of our current illiteracy.

Direct literacy as regards natural phenomena is required as we grapple with the threat of floods and storms. Among the people who survived the South-east Asian tsunami were individuals who had learned during geography lessons at school, that a retreat of the sea will be followed by a reciprocal surge in the sea level. They had managed to flee the coastal regions earlier than many of those who did not survive the tsunami. We are surrounded by technology, systems and knowledge that can predict and communicate many things, but in addition to these things, both understanding of phenomena and skills to utilise technology have to be developed.

Corporate Literacy fosters the use and spreading of essential and accurate information and the learning of organisational processes. It helps the organisations to identify future risks and possibilities, as well as the consequences of their operations upon the environment. This kind of information can more broadly be viewed as a key component in the transfer to sustainable development. The world needs a societal balance, both socially and economically. The literacy of companies and societies includes the ability to read both nature and the surrounding world with its economic and social structures and to take proper responsibility for their actions and the consequences of these actions.

## Managing in the networked information environment

It is debatable whether we actually live in an information society, whether an information society is basically that much different from other societies or whether existing in an information society has changed human beings fundamentally. However, it is undeniable that information and networking are important features of modern society, business, work and daily life in many parts of the world. Information and

Communication Technology has been the engine driving forward this development and appears to be leading us on to a future that offers amazing opportunities, opportunities that companies aim to commercialise into products for consumer use.

Goal-oriented activities in this information and networking environment are so demanding that companies and public administration must create a new kind of literacy that helps them to orientate and operate in this environment, setting and achieving their own goals. If an organisation does not develop its literacy, it will float hopelessly on the surface of a sea of information, being tossed about amid all the new possibilities without ever understanding where it is heading. Corporate Literacy helps to connect new information with a wider context and background: knowledge based on experience and future visions from the perspective of the company's own goals. This process is in principle, the same as in the case of a wise thinking individual interpreting new information, but Corporate Literacy is formed based on the goals of the organisation and there are more resources than in the case of an individual for the formation of a joint literacy.

## The information-based environment

What kind of an environment is the information and networked society? Its features include the complexity and unpredictability referred to, and discussed in the previous chapter, as being features of the global operational environment.

Books in high-quality bookshops laid out on promotional stands to attract the consumer, present a good window through which to read the world. The information-based environment around us is illustrated by the fact that these windows are to be found everywhere. Media, newspaper headlines, street adverts, the Internet and mobile services offer continuous information and messages, weighing down human consciousness and thought and making it difficult to pick out the critical issues. In an urban environment, a person is targeted daily by approximately 2000 messages or product brands. There is no need to seek information as it surrounds us, particularly in an urban environment. The most visible messages are mainly commercial, but social advertising is also widely displayed. Advertising has also become information-based. Advertising offers further information relating to products and services via www addresses. These different windows to information vary as regards their quality. It is also increasingly difficult to distinguish advertising content from journalistic content. This is particularly the case, on the Internet, where it is all mixed together. Information genres (for example, information relating to authorities, research, sales and personal opinions) are difficult to distinguish from each other and the biographical and source information is often inadequate. The parties receiving the messages are often dependent on their own level of literacy when evaluating the content and meaning of the information offered, as well as its connection with reality.

The amount of information grows exponentially: it has been calculated to double its current level in about 3 years. Berkeley University has calculated that at the turn of the twenty-first century people and their machines produced, in the space of 3 years, more information than during the preceding 300,000 years (Lyman and Varian 2003). The amount of the information produced is unbelievable and it exists both in digital and paper form. What do people pick up from this flow of messages and information? How do they even cope within this over-flowing environment?

It is generally agreed that the amount of information *per se* will not provide solutions or help in anything. The amount of information indeed, in and of itself, causes problems. People are suffering from informational overload and from a constant feeling of insecurity that the most essential information is still beyond their grasp. This information bombardment threatens the ability of the brain to function. Information exhaustion is the new occupational illness of today. On the other hand, those, such as the elderly persons, who are not participating in this information environment may feel excluded and as a result, increasingly insecure. Many people, irrespective of their living circumstances, share the experience of feeling unable to take hold of their daily lives and maintain an acceptable degree of control over their daily lives.

Informational overload affects ordinary citizens, workers and top-level decision-makers of companies and societies. The issue is very serious once one sees that the basis of these activities and decision-making processes is the need for information. Information technology is a tool and it alone will not provide solutions for a long time to come. Rather, what we need to be concerned with is finding meaning in content and honing our ability to do so. The results of genetic research and daily chats are both handled by the computers in the same way: as bit queues. A person reading the same information will interpret and evaluate, in ways appropriate to the differing characteristics of the two sets of information. The evaluation of the meaning and content remains in the domain of human ability.

The amount of information as such does not help us to make good decisions and to operate wisely. However, a large amount of information offers a wide range of selection: information expressing different views; information produced from different perspectives; research results from different schools and fields; information interpreted by different interest groups. We must not only improve the way in which we select, from the large amount of available, we must also evaluate and analyse the information selected.

## Information flow expands the range of intellectual enquiry

Abundant information is also a tremendous resource. In his book, relating to the history of civilisation Douglas S. Robertson (1998) concluded that civilisations are generally information-limited. According to him, sudden and unpredictable information flow (not all of it 'right' information, far from it, in fact) was limited, even in the heyday of the renaissance. The reason for achievements in arts, science, trade and commerce were not so much to do with human genius, but rather the growth of information that was suddenly within the reach of a greater number of people. Print media offered people information they were hungry for as well as the possibility to transmit ideas and innovations to much greater numbers of people much more rapidly than ever before. The first generation producing books on any significant scale also participated in foreign expeditions. For example, the generation that duplicated books by Marco Polo, travelled to find new worlds. The generation that printed Copernicus' *De Revolutionibus*, started to question theories associated with the essential nature of the universe. A large amount of information will no doubt arouse new questions and expand the range of intellectual enquiry.

With the growth in the amount of information, scientific methods have always been developed simultaneously for processing these large amounts of information. The quality of even the publications produced by early printing technology was criticised as a large part of the printed information was incorrect and non-scientific. The amount of this non-scientific information was greatly reduced with the development of printing technology. Serious reports relating to dragons, which were first used to deceive people who believed unquestioningly in the written word, were becoming rare as early as the seventeenth century. At least part of the answer is found in the development of the scientific methods of the fifteenth and the sixteenth century. The methods were developed alongside the growth in the amount of information.

A direct analogy can be found between the state of affairs as described above and the world we now inhabit. Currently we are developing a semantic web, which would ease the filtering of relevant information from the abundance of information on the Internet. Search engines are being developed. The human genotype is fully mapped. Scientific discoveries and innovations are created when information from different fields is combined. The abundance of information may help us to eventually solve many of our current problems. Therefore, it is crucially important that companies and public administration bodies develop skills and methods for the effective selection, analysis, interpretation and communication of information. Well-selected information is an auxiliary on our journey forward like compasses, maps and stars are to the seafarer. We have to learn to navigate this information-rich environment. Along with the development of our literacy, we will also gain new understandings and make new discoveries and innovations.

Development within the fields of information and networking has progressed, simultaneously, and each serves to promote the other. The Internet, World Wide Web and search engines have together facilitated access to a wide range of information resources and publications, as well as the rapid distribution of, and searching for, information. Networks are also a communication environment. Depending from which perspective the Internet is being viewed; it can be described as a virtual market-place or memory. In addition to being an information environment, it is also an operational, communication and learning environment.

The development of information and networking continues and is also reaching utilities, clothing, public facilities and homes. It might be that in the future every person and item has an URL address. Wireless Internet connections can be used in almost any facility. This will make it possible at any time to obtain information about almost any object. One needs to ask: What is this information about, who produces it and what is it based on? It will also be possible to collect more information about people and their behaviour. Corporate Literacy involves taking responsibility for the information companies or other organisations produce and collect in terms of accuracy, quality of information and data protection. Organisations have to improve their Corporate Literacy significantly, in order to be able to utilise large-scale information resources and identify opportunities, as well as the dangers and threats connected with the ubiquitous networking processes.

How do the managing directors of large international companies and presidents of states manage the information flood? Their mental capacity may not be significantly any greater than any citizen's, even though they may have, due to their background, a lot of knowledge, experience and expertise. Behind their decisions exists a corporate body, which reads the world and filters and prioritises issues using the methods of the specific organisational information and decision-making cultures. In addition, they have their personal channels, reading methods and techniques: confidential experts and information sources, contacts and networks.

Information behind the decision-making process is formed via many steps and networks by combining materials from different sources so that actual information sources, opinion leaders and the role of the decision-maker is difficult to identify and distinguish within the decision-making process. When the aim is to make a decision on information the decision-maker may often find it difficult to assess in practice when there is a sufficient amount of information available. Information may not necessarily lead to certainty within the decision-making process but may on the contrary cause significant insecurity. If a high-level of Corporate Literacy supports the decision-maker, it may not make the decision-making process any easier, but the basis for information will be reliable.

Even if the leaders have a reliable corporate background, it is still no guarantee of its having a highly developed Corporate Literacy. Leaders, past and present, have followed a decision-making process based on the interests and literacy level of a small group of people. Both companies and public administrations draw wrong conclusions about the opinions of citizens. The development of networking and information has increased the possibilities for citizens to obtain information and expanded their literacy skills. Enlightened citizens and their organisations watch the activities of companies, public administrations and politicians.

Corporate Literacy supports a versatile shared development based on dialogue. The clarification of difficult issues requires teams specifically set up for this purpose, where the participants represent different fields and view the problem concerned from different angles. The formation of these teams and the tuning of their motivation to work requires, as such, an understanding of the problem as a whole and an ability to look at it from different aspects. Corporate Literacy supports a goal-oriented method of working where the aim is to utilise information for finding solutions. The difference with typical teamwork is that the assembly of the team-members is undertaken by people representing different skills and fields. In order to solve the target problem, information based on different fields and perspectives is applied and working methods promoting shared problem-solving processes are used. Information professionals should develop their skills as the promoters of this kind of working, as creators of teams representing multilevel information, as experts in working methods and as builders of Corporate Literacy.

## Towards Comprehensive Literacy

Information is flowing everywhere. We get information from everything that can be seen, heard, smelled, tasted, felt physically or perceived mentally. The senses can be left in state of closure; they can be numbed and left undernourished. Shared Corporate Literacy is based on the locating and the skilled use of these shared senses by all the corporate members. Corporate Literacy is visual, auditory and kinetic. It is a multisemiotic and multimodular skill. It can be applied to text, speech, visual images and sound messages and it can recognise the meaning of gestures and movements. It is not innate to individuals anymore than to organisations, but is instead, a result of perception, learning and practice. Our senses and cells provide us with foundations for the development of our literacy skills. Findings from brain research over the last 10 years have included the mirror cells, which, quick as lightning, tune us into the feelings of others. A better understanding about the mechanism of our senses and mutual communication may also aid us in the shared processing of large amounts of information.

Literacy means the recognition of meanings and the knowledge of meanings requires learning. As the information environment is multisemiotic or multimodular, all the senses are needed for the recognition of meanings. We also know that the current learning concepts emphasise communality. According to Ralph Stacey 'learning is the activity of interdependent people and can only be understood in terms of self-organising communicative interaction and power relating in which identities are potentially transformed.' (Stacey 2003).

Just like the individual, all organisations and companies as well as public organisations and communities, need a collaborative Corporate Literacy. Via literacy an organisation evaluates, filters and browses information and knowledge. *Via literacy, an organisation redefines itself continuously.*

## Discovering the senses: finding the meaning

From the beginning of their existence, human beings have had the skill to observe their environment and make observations about it. This skill is used to find good dwelling places, food, to catch prey, to sense danger and to take flight in time. In natural surroundings, the senses were practised in observing and interpreting natural phenomena. The skill to read written text expanded the common memory, the sharing of experiences and knowledge and possibilities for learning. The eyes were opened to look beyond the immediate environment at the world beyond possibilities latent there. Social contracts and legislation were tied to the written language enabling the birth of civilisation.

Based on current knowledge the skill of writing was invented about 5000 years independently in different parts of the world, for example in Mesopotamia, Egypt, China and Central America as part of cultural development. Gutenberg's printing technology revolutionised the possibilities for the distribution of information about 600 years ago. Written communications first as printed products, and nowadays via information technology, have facilitated the rapid global spread of information. Text, pictures and sound can be transmitted via various communication equipment and channels all over the world within a few seconds. However, it should be remembered that even in the twenty-first century there are still hundreds of millions of illiterate adults in the world. At the turn of the twenty-first century approximately 15% of over 15-year-old males and approximately 26% of females were illiterate. Regional differences are large. In some countries over half of the women are illiterate, whereas in the European Union countries only 1% of men and only 2% of women are illiterate. Significantly, along with the diffusion of the new media there is an increasing and contradictory trend of neo-illiteracy in industrialised countries. The amount of neo-illiterates is estimated to be about 10–15% of the adult population. These individuals have great difficulties managing daily tasks, such as the use of credit cards and bus timetables.

Modern literacy skills can be seen as a multiple extension, which relates to total information acquisition, filtering, interpretation, production, communication and legal and ethical process, irrespective of the technical or media form. In addition, literacy can be viewed laterally in the different areas of information: literacy skills relating to different areas of science, statistics, finance, advertising, politics, religions, etc.

Attention has been paid to Information Literacy, particularly in higher education. An information literate individual is able to:

■ determine the extent of information needed;

- access the needed information effectively and efficiently;

- evaluate information and its sources critically;

- incorporate selected information into one's knowledge base;

- use information effectively to accomplish a specific purpose;

- understand the economic, legal and social issues surrounding the use of information and access and use information ethically and legally (see reference, American Library Association).

Information Literacy has been defined broadly above but it is strongly accentuated from the perspective of library operations for information searches and the assessment of information sources.

The following definition has the same content but emphasises more attitudes, learning and use of information according to which an information-literate person:

- engages in independent, self-directed learning;

- uses information processes;

- uses a variety of information technologies and systems;

- has internalised values that promote information use;

- has a sound knowledge of the world of information;

- approaches information critically;

- has a personal information style that facilitates his or her interaction with the world of information (Bawden and Robinson 2001).

Media Literacy is being discussed within the fields of communication, communication research and teaching and covers mainly similar areas. In addition, Media Literacy emphasises both multisemiotic or multimodular media techniques and media elements (picture, sound, cuts) and skills to communicate, produce and publish the content. The importance of understanding different cultures, religions and value systems and social competence are emphasised within the global operational environment (Varis 2005).

Literacy of social structures has become more difficult in the global world where the locality of administration and power often are not very clear. Specialisation of different fields and different concepts has made it more difficult to read, understand and interpret the information contents of different fields. Ordinary citizens need literacy relating to economics, politics, jurisprudence, science, the natural environment and different cultures and religions. The level of standards within companies and public administrations is higher than ever and grows as citizen awareness. Organisations, companies and public administrations require a high-level of Customer Literacy.

The concept of literacy includes responsibility, awareness and the ability to take into account ethical, social and judicial factors associated with information attainment and production. Responsibility as regards information is emphasised in the network environment where in principle, anybody can publish almost anything without any verification.

In Spring 2005 I was listening to a debate between a communication researcher and a journalist where the topic of the discussion was 'Media, citizens and power'. The debate was bouncing back and forth until the meaning of social literacy popped up. This surprisingly unified the views of the parties as regards what a society needs to ensure democracy and the interpretation of information transmitted by the media. Skills are needed for the interpretation of communication backgrounds and an understanding of the decision-making process, complex social and economic structures and meanings.

## New kinds of structures, new information flows

Organisational literacy can also be viewed, on this basis, as a continuously changing, dynamic and interactive process of people operating together. Common, continuously changing knowledge and the learning of new things is based on this literacy. Via its common literacy a corporate body with partners, receives information, communicates with its partners and environment and influences it in the form of its products, services, decisions or other activities. Through its literacy, a corporate body defines what it considers information and will continuously reconstruct it. The development of Corporate Literacy is a practical way to function as regards information but we still do not understand its deep, scientific nature.

The gap between those who are highly literate and those who are still illiterate will continue to grow apace, unless we take strong action to rectify the situation. In countries where there is a strong movement for development it may be possible to move straight to the broadly based literacy required by the globally networked operational environment. Experiences of others can be fully utilised and yet one's own, creative and innovative operational models can be developed. The development of broadly-based literacy, which utilises information technology in companies and local organisations, could result in a big leap towards economic and social progress, if local and global resources can be linked creatively based on specific background and set goals. The 'flatness' of the globe in the information and communication technology sense and even in the economic sense will lead to great changes much faster than we are able to realise: in fact, while we are sleeping as Friedman describes in his book *The World is Flat* (Friedman 2005). The consequence is that work, expertise and economic growth are being divided in a new way. The USA is in a new competitive situation. Europe worries about the ageing of its population and fears becoming just a tourist destination for history buffs. The availability of information resources, broadly speaking gives local corporate bodies and communities much more powerful potential resources than they have had before.

## Literacy skills in a multisemiotic information environment

Written communication has had a significant role in the world of science and communications ever since the invention of printing technology. However, modern information transmission is in reality mainly a multisemiotic information flow in text, pictures, sounds, scents and smells. Advertising effectively utilises pictures, movements, sounds and scents but even in the transmission of news the effect of the pictures is significant both in the television and newspapers, and even more so, on the Internet.

Traditionally text has been thought of as written and also spoken language. Gradually it was perceived that language is not the only element via which text communicates. For example, the illustration of a newspaper article and web page has an important role. Philologists, among others, perceive illustration to be as part of the text, not a separate surrounding factor. A newspaper article or web page is seen as being formed by the writing and illustration, which together form the text. These two cannot be separated from each other or put into any order of importance.

In addition to visual presentations and written texts, multisemiotic texts can also contain sound, animation and videos. From the perspective of literacy, the understanding of the networked information environment as being multisemiotic is essential. Comprehensive literacy includes the ability to read multisemiotic texts.

The literacy of individuals is often limited. People representing different professional fields and different generations have literacy and information habits that have developed and accentuated differently. For many years, I have been involved in training information professionals in various information and communication training programmes within university adult education. The participants being trained have represented graduates working within the field of information or communications. Their academic backgrounds have varied from information technology and engineering to humanistic, social and natural sciences. The different sciences emphasise numeric, written, visual or sound-based information. The limitation of literacy in a certain type of information can clearly be seen, based on their university background, in the work the participants produce as exercises. My close colleagues share this view. If we are used to interpret phenomena and to communicate, for example, in the form of texts, our literacy level to read numerically or visually represented text and also the transmission of information using these methods may be very poor.

In my training activities, I have found that the majority of the information professionals have emphasised written literacy. They are skilled in analysing issues via text and prefer communication via written texts. The visual outlining of issues is not developed or natural. Those outlining issues visually are still a minority among the information professionals.

The field of communications has its own specialists for written, visual and sound communications: journalists, graphic artists, visual artists and sound designers. Within films and multimedia the director and producer assemble the work by them. Lawyers preparing legislation work mainly with texts. However, all the communicative and functional elements including physical items and any traces in them are analysed in crime investigations. Doctors and nurses have to be able to 'read' not just the patient directly but they also have to be able to interpret any documented medical information and laboratory samples for their diagnosis. Most editors are comfortable with written material and interviews with people but need Statistical Literacy. Researchers depending on their field of science and expertise have often studied analysis and interpretation of either quantitative or qualitative material. Ethnography is an example of a field using various different research methods simultaneously (interviews, stories, drawings, participatory observation, video filming, recordings, artefacts, etc.) and truly utilises multisemiotic literacy in its broadest meaning.

Information professionals should work within the multisemiotic environment to overcome their limitations within the form of information when obtaining, interpreting and distributing information. They should also be professionals in their information, media and multilevel literacy.

Depending on the perspective and task of the user of the information, other differences also exist in literacy habits and requirements. The professionals and organisations offering information have to be aware of these differences. It all depends on what level of depth information is required. Researchers need information relating to the background and methods. Busy company directors and administrative decision-makers want to have access to research results and effective information as such. The difference is whether what are needed are accurate facts in a brief form or a drawn out series or broad background information, perhaps even within the softening and enchanting glow of a story or cartoon.

Finnish opera singer Matti Salminen analysed his classically based but almost 'omnivorous' musical preferences by stating that music to him is any music with a distinguished melodic message. He also said that in his opinion the majority of the pop and rock music listened to by the youth is not this kind of music. He only hears pop and rock as mere noise. However, he also stated that the youth are likely to have an ability distinguish the music from this noise: an ability to read this music. Equally a person not used to listening to classical music, may hear it as a mixed flow of tones and the singing of a soprano even as 'shrieking'. Where one person hears just noise, another is able to distinguish a message, melody and harmony. In semiotics, a sound is a signifier that like rock may symbolise noise for some people, whereas to some others it may symbolise purpose of life or an interesting social phenomenon. Equally the background and the level of literacy of a person determine what the person concerned interprets as information. This is also applicable to Corporate Literacy. It can be developed further to hear new kinds of 'sounds'.

Different literacy skills represent wealth. Organisations need multisemiotic and multilevel literacy. All organisations have more of this kind of literacy than they are aware. It is present in their staff representing people of different ages, different kinds of education, work experience and personal backgrounds and skills, in their networks and in their different information and communication environments. Corporate

Literacy should be constructed by valuing and listening to these differences.

## Customer Literacy

Understanding the needs and wishes of customers is an essential part of Corporate Literacy. The customer-oriented approach is a matter of course to a village shopkeeper who knows all the customers and takes care of their various needs. With the growth of the sizes of companies and the complexity of business, the customer has become a distant and anonymous target. However, these 'targets' are thinking and functioning people and their actions cannot be that easily controlled.

The collection of information relating to customers, their needs, expectations and feedback and also the whole of Customer Relationship Management is seen as the foundation pillar, which could be developed systematically, with information systems also developed for it. Customer information collected and researched by different units of the company can be combined via technology for utilisation in the decision-making process. Along with the company's own processes, it is also possible to study the processes of customers and find there objects for product development.

Customer-awareness has increased significantly. People want more information about the products they buy, their production processes and the operational methods of companies. With the abundance of information available on the Internet, people are able to make comparisons between companies. The Internet enables the fast flow of information and allows access to alternative information in addition to the information offered by the company itself. Customers can join forces and establish consumer associations, distribute information and build up international networks. Global citizen movements take a stand on both the global trading and ethical operational methods of companies and environmental effects. People also demonstrate against states by boycotting products originating in the states concerned. The boycotting can be easily spread via Internet and text messaging. As an example is, also in this context, the speedily spread boycotting of Danish products within the Islamic states as a demonstration against the publication of the cartoon showing Prophet Muhammad.

Literacy levels of the 'new' customers are broad. As customers, they are restless, swift-moving and strong opinion creators within their own environments. In addition to the features of the product, they also see in the product the production chain and social and environmental effects it represents. The customers expect the companies to be open and transparent in these matters.

When collecting information about their customers the companies have to remember to respect their privacy and data protection. People are increasingly more aware about the fact that information is being gathered about them using loyalty cards and cookies located on web pages. Not all accept this collection of information. When information is collected it has to take place in accordance with the law, transparently and based on permission from the customers. Care has to be taken that the information in the data systems is correct and updated and cannot be forwarded without the permission of the customer. If a company is careless or indifferent in these matters it will at some point be penalised by a loss of customers. Operations on the Internet require high literacy levels from the company as regards the customers, markets, network features and jurisprudence. Corporate Literacy formed from attention to and the linking of different aspects and expertise of different fields is necessary within the network environment.

## *Phenomena beneath the surface*

The 'iceberg' phenomenon where only a small part of the whole is visible is an interesting metaphor when thinking of our information environment. It is worthwhile for the organisations to pay attention to it from the perspective of their own literacy. Operations on the surface seem fairly smooth but the depth dimension may bring along matters we may crash into unless we identify the threat in time. New material is occasionally being brought to the surface from the depths, like in a volcanic eruption. The material may provide the ingredients for renewal and for the creation of new things but it may also have destructive consequences. The contradictory relationship of the visible surface and the processes deep underneath creates tension that has to be discharged at some point. A tsunami is created by submerged continental drift. Ships sailing the seas are not able to identify a surge moving underneath them with a speed that may be as much as, 800 kilometres/hour, which, upon reaching the shore is capable of producing a 50-metre high wall of water. The results of human actions, as witnessed in New York on 11 September 2001 and the bomb strikes in London in 2005, not to mention in past revolutions and wars, reflect social tensions, boiling to the surface and thence exploding skywards, like molten lava erupting from a volcano.

We need to ask what is going on underneath the surface and to search for information that is not immediately visible and easily available. Deep currents are moving below the instantly accessible information: slow information inside human beings, inside the organisation, not to mention the various processes between different cultures. While debating these matters we need to listen and also try to find out what deeper meanings and processes exist beyond the speech and ask ourselves what might be coming. Literacy means – when facing incomprehensible phenomena – an ability to ask: What do you want to express by this? The greater the differences in cultural background, history and circumstance, the more attentive we need to be when listening.

This kind of information attainment method, where in addition to instant current information, attention is paid to deeper level informational structures, can be developed to a systematic level. In acute situations it requires attention to, and checking of, the different dimensions of information both in daily and exceptional circumstances.

## From passive reception to conscious attention

As a consequence of large amounts of information, haste and short-term action we receive easily accessible surface information without analysing it, without checking the sources and without thinking any further. People have a tendency toward a firm belief in the information they read or hear first even though it might later prove incorrect. People also have a tendency to select information which strengthen their own personally held opinions and reinforce their own value system and views. This relates as much to political decision-makers, company directors and ordinary citizens as to journalists providing instant information. Information providers may be quite purpose-oriented but the receiving parties are vulnerable to manipulation and disinformation. The same people and corporations can act both as information providers and information receivers.

If we don't have any conscious selection and filtering mechanisms our brains and thoughts will get filled with the headings of the tabloid papers, rally drivers' romances and tragedies of princesses or with disinformation. Our thinking and perceptions about the world are guided by obscure surface information, which in reality has nothing to do with our own environment, our work and our goals. Our thought energy is used for engagement with an environment full of sex and violence even if we consciously would not wish it to be so.

Professor Stephan Lewandowsky from the Western Australian University specialised in psychology has studied the persistence of incorrect information by looking into what people remember from the Iraqi war (Lewandowsky *et al.* 2005). People who believed that the war was fought because of the weapons of mass destruction did not update their views to match the corrected information. Many of them even thought that they remembered that weapons of mass destruction had really been found in Iraq. The continuous bombarding by the media relating to the suspicions remained in people's minds and became a fact.

It was written in *Newsweek* on 9 May 2005 that the paper had been informed by governmental sources that Muslim prisoners in Guantanamo had been forced to desecrate the Koran. The news was cancelled on 15 May as it was not possible to prove the event but the cancellation was not believed with the consequence that the whole Muslim world was inflamed.

Incorrect information cannot be corrected just by commenting that 'it wasn't correct' without giving any grounds for it. According to Lewandowsky et al. (2005), correction is possible only by using deeper information, by stating the reason and consequent relations of the process of the event.

In practice nobody is able to check all the information provided or to check thoroughly the processes in the background. We have to be selective as regards the issues we become engaged in and what kind of matters we want to have knowledge of. When we are busy and uncertain serious errors can take place as a consequence of surface information. The most important thing both in organisations and on an individual level is consciously to select the essential areas of information where the desired correct information and knowledge can be obtained. By developing Corporate Literacy it is possible to obtain more resources and foster a capacity to gain knowledge relating to these important issues, than is the case when everybody is trying to achieve this by themselves.

## Responsibility for information necessary, control of information impossible

The information professionals, both journalists and information specialists carry a particularly great responsibility for not forwarding unreliable surface information. In practice this approach is easily ignored. In the case of journalists, this is made difficult by the commercial goals of the media. Both of these professional groups are 'time poor' just like many others. Changing of corporate information behaviour via every individual, the development of common critical literacy and information production practices is the only way forward. The quality of information is not any more just a matter for the professionals but concerns all the users and providers of information. Information is 'material' we all use and work with. Each said and written sentence whether erroneous or true can start moving forwards from here particularly if it is found on the Internet. In the modern information environment and particularly on the Internet incorrect information easily and speedily multiplies and is difficult to trace and correct afterwards. Responsibility for information at the initial stages is necessary, control of information impossible.

Monitoring and censoring any information is increasingly

more difficult in the open and multichannelled network environment. The effort by the Chinese authorities to control the flow of information with the help of 30,000 Internet police is likely to fail even if supported by an advanced information filtering system. There is always a channel somewhere for information and new ones are created all the time. Responsibility for information cannot be established by force it has to be based on the free will of the people. Responsibility for information has to be supported by the corporate body. Responsibility for information is part of Corporate Literacy.

An ability to read and evaluate information produced by the environment gives a basis for building a new type of order for information: to analyse and organise information resources and to provide knowledge for the use of others. A new way to read the environment will unavoidably lead to a new way to organise information so that it can be approached from different aspects and for different needs. Information architecture in of the organisations should be constructed on this basis.

The more skilled an organisation is in reading and decoding the network information environment and its complex information sources and contents, the better it is able to form the required information basis and to anticipate changes. Within this process the organisation also learns to offer and transmit information to customers, citizens and partners in a usable form. Corporate Literacy will be part of the special know-how and development of the organisation itself.

# 2

# Corporate Literacy in practice

## Steps towards Corporate Literacy

What does Corporate Literacy consist of in practice? How can progress be made towards it? How can the senses of the organisation be discovered? How can an enterprise, public administration unit or some target-oriented society achieve the comprehensive literacy required in our ever-changing, less than secure, operational environment? John Unsworth argues that the notion of literacy needs to be conceptualised as a plurality of literacies, and *becoming* literate is a more apt expression than *being* literate (Varis 2006). This applies also to Corporate Literacy. An organisation has to construct the learning process of multifield literacy while being aware of the requirements and desired goals.

We are talking about the development of a new type of information culture within an organisation. While up until the present, plenty of energy has been used on information administration and technology, it is now important to focus on the information itself and exactly what information is important.

The corporate process of becoming literate has four important sectors, which need to be developed together with an awareness of their joint importance.

1. *Strategy*: the creation of an information strategy; where to focus attention.

2. *Channels*: identification and tuning of the senses, development and utilisation of versatile literacy; how the organisation reads its environment.

3. *Architecture*: construction of information architecture supporting comprehensive literacy; creation and reconstruction of structures for information flows.

4. *Method of operation*: empowering and sharing; development of a culture enabling changes in attitudes and operations.

Information technology, the Internet and mobile communication are used widely all over the world. The visions of an information and even knowledge society have been refined over the last 20 years. Organisations have developed information resources management, information and Knowledge Management, business intelligence, data mining, document management and content management as well as concepts such as emotional intelligence. However, when discussing the information of organisations the prevailing language has been the language of technology and administration. Now the question of exactly which information and why has to be revealed by drawing the veil of the language of technology. Companies, public administration and political decision-makers have to face massive challenges to resolve problems relating to globalisation, climate change, economic, social and health issues. We need higher levels of literacy as citizens, consumers and companies. Organisational information structures have to be renovated, as the operational and information environments are new and many of the parties concerned have not kept pace with change. This has led to problems when interacting with the external world and rapidly progressing events.

The decisions concerning the planned development of Corporate Literacy and its primary targets have to be taken by the management of the organisation. The development of organisational literacy relates to the whole organisation, its structures and operational methods.

## Which are the fields and forms of information an organisation should be able to read?

The more abundant and variable the information environment is the more awareness it requires from the organisation, as well as from individuals, as regards its own goals. What are the issues we follow? Where do we focus our attention? Which issues do we need to develop a deeper understanding of than currently exists? What information do we share and pass on? People have never before experienced the current information and communication environment and therefore advanced selection abilities have not been required. On the other hand, nature itself offers an equally abundant information environment requiring a highly developed awareness; an ability to remain continually alert and select appropriate information in order to facilitate survival based on nature's terms. Why should we not learn to apply these abilities to the current information environment?

The creation of Corporate Literacy requires that the whole organisation has a vision and awareness of what information is important to it. The organisation has to implement a collectively adopted information strategy. We are talking about a significantly more difficult matter than information technology strategy or strategies aimed at the control of the form of information. It is possible we may also meet a situation in which we are not sure what information is important. However, this should not lead to a situation where we will be drifting in an expanding information flow, which we try to control without any sense of purpose.

An organisation focuses its attention and selects information utilising the information strategy. Therefore the organisation should decide which information should be easily accessible to everybody in the 'surface net' and which information should be lifted from the 'deep net' to be made visible using systematic procedures. It has to be decided, based on the strategy, what form of information resources the organisation is going to create for itself and how the various information materials link to each other. The information strategy guides the information and knowledge processes supporting the operations of the organisation.

In information strategy a stand has to be taken as regards information content and quality: what information is important, what kind of criteria is set for this information and how is this information obtained and distributed. From the standpoint of Corporate Literacy the determination of important information areas is a primary matter. If important information areas are not determined, it may be that in making decisions for the future, attention is not given to some essential matters. Even the largest organisations are managed by human beings who are restricted by human limits when making decisions. The effect could result in a certain significant issue being left without attention. When dealing with globalisation and economic issues, for example, environmental issues may be forgotten even though they may have a significant economic effect. When the information strategy is given careful thought and action is taken accordingly, literacy is aimed at all relevant areas identified as being of possible import or significance. Then they can also be taken into account in decision-making and activities deriving from the decision-making process.

Information strategy is a tool for management and is the responsibility of management but its implementation requires acceptance and internalisation by the whole organisation. If positive conditions are created for the utilisation of information and information resources and flows are organised based on a common strategy, the paralysing information overloading and anxieties to manage the workload are reduced. When we know where attention should be focused, it releases resources for important tasks and improves the performance of people.

There is no information without communication. No information system should be constructed without taking into account the communication factors. An organisation should do its best to ensure that its employees are supported by a good communication environment. A joint information and communication strategy enables a framework for the construction of a long-term information and communication environment and the development of Corporate Literacy.

## Structuring an information strategy: finding the language of knowledge

The starting points for an information strategy include a vision, a task and an operational strategy. Within an information strategy they are taken from the point of view of information: which information is needed for implementation of the vision and the strategy.

Information strategy relates to the whole organisation. Therefore it should be understood and adopted by everybody. The grounding of the information strategy should incorporate the views of the management, the operational units and their experts. Information strategy is not the business of information technology, information systems, information services or those responsible for Knowledge Management or Information Management; they can only have a role as technical support in the implementation of information strategy. The language of knowledge is different to the language of technology, systems or management.

The first stage for structuring an information strategy is an analysis of the organisational vision and strategy and an interpretation from the perspective of information. Thought must be given to what the goals set for the organisation mean from the perspective of information and what elements do they provide for the information strategy. Irrespective of whose task it is in practice to construct the information strategy, the initial discussion has to take place with the senior management. The main question in this discussion is: what information is important for the realisation of the vision and strategy of the organisation?

The information strategy deals not with information management but with knowledge itself and the question asked is not *How?* but rather, *What?*. The language has to reflect as well and as accurately as possible the work and realities present within the organisation. The language of information strategy should describe the reality so that it can be understood by all the people working within the organisation. Commercial language, which is used for sales, also has to be eliminated from the information strategy. This makes it possible to reach the core concepts of the organisation and, via this route, on to core matters and core knowledge. Literacy means that the language of knowledge expressing what it really is all about is retrieved from beneath the languages and terminologies of specific businesses, marketing, advertising, politics, jurisprudence, science, technology and economics. This is the language the information strategy of the organisation must use.

The information strategy must also be able to answer the question, *Why?* When information strategy is structured according to the vision and strategy of the organisation, the solution can be found within it. Building upon a sustainable basis is vital if the organisation is to have a meaningful foundation and the information strategy is to have a solid grounding.

In the same way as the organisation has to identify its core activities and core processes, it has to identify the core information. Core information can be gathered internally within the organisation or produced outside the organisation, including observations or researched information relating to its own activities or to the world outside. Core information can on the one hand be outlined as a view of important information areas and on the other hand as knowledge and information flows to and from the processes and tasks of the organisation.

## *Horizontal view of the information pertaining to the organisation: knowledge map*

An overall horizontal view relating to the information landscape of the organisation has to be created in order to construct an information strategy. A knowledge map of an organisation is a demonstrative tool to help form a common understanding relating to and between the strategic information areas. A map enables the formation of a visual representation of the strategic information areas of the organisation. Using the map it is possible to discuss and assess which of the information areas are strong, which are weak and which should be focused on in the information strategy.

The first draft of the knowledge map involves mapping the landscape: the information areas that belong to the information environment of the organisation are outlined. The next stage is the selection of strategic information areas. Too detailed an inspection should be avoided in the initial stages in order to lay out the strategic outlines. When the information areas are identified and drafted in black and white it is important that fundamental discussions relating to the information and the status of information management are activated. It is important to document these discussions. Discussions are carried out and documented as long as it has been possible to identify the strategic information areas accurately, the knowledge map seems ready and it has the approval of the management. After that it is important to apply substantial consideration to visualisation. A professional in visual design should create a knowledge map that is memorable, clear and applicable: providing a representation of the organisational culture; a shared information tool; and an aid to communication. It is important that the map is visible via the intranet and other shared facilities. The map is needed for the development of the organisation and for the planning of the information architecture, information systems and network services.

The knowledge map is a visual description of the essential information areas of the organisation. It shows which aspects require attention and focuses the Corporate Literacy to target these areas. It is taken to practical levels by deepening the viewing of the map to how and where the information relating to each is available and what should be done to develop each information area.

When attention within the organisation using visualisation focuses on certain areas, it is possible to start to identify new connections and new issues relating to these. When these observations and ideas are shared within the organisation, the understanding relating to the information and knowledge is deepened and expanded.

| Figure 2.1 | Mapping the information and knowledge landscape of a company |

## *Vertical literacy: twisted processes*

Literacy also has to be developed within the processes of the organisation. If we call the mapping described above, outlining information areas, a horizontal view into information, we could talk about vertical literacy in connection with the processes.

Vertical literacy means that information and knowledge processes and flows are formed and developed for the support of operational processes. The identification, outlining and separation of information and knowledge processes have proven to be difficult both in practice and theory. The processes overlap each other. Within an information-intensive environment, information or knowledge processes can be the same as the operational process or a part of it.

It is typical of the working methods of an information society that the vertical processes are flattened so that many operations are undertaken simultaneously. The processes still exist but they are twisted and curled over a short time period, furthermore, the flow of the processes cannot be determined in advance. The process, for example, will twist into a cell where the professionals and experts representing different fields are engaged in a joint task. In such a case, all of the information required for the processes has to be available all of the time. Cell-based working means cell-based literacy.

An information strategy and the literacy based on it have to be constructed in accordance with the organisation's own working and operational practices.

## The surface and depth level of literacy

The information strategy must highlight not only the matter and phenomena attention is to be focused on, but also to which depth level they are to be monitored and analysed. It is a different objective to pick up signals from continuous news' flow than to gain a well-grounded understanding about some entity, its reasons, consequences and effects. Sifting essential information will become increasingly laborious as the growth of disinformation is even greater than the growth of information based on facts. The speed of information is important for the decision-making process of companies as well as social and political decision-making, but in addition, more slowly accrued understanding, based on information gleaned via thorough research and evaluation and taking into consideration various perspectives is equally important. In activities based on information a balance between these two levels is required: fast surface monitoring and the application of in-depth knowledge.

The continuous flow of new issues and concepts creates a strain at work in modern organisations and particularly with information-based work, where occasionally it turns into an avalanche of concepts. People are exposed to thousands of messages in their daily workplaces, which contain concepts they don't understand or that require considerable effort to understand. This takes place in meetings, discussions, networking, when in contact with professionals representing different fields, when using a computer, mobile phones and information systems required for work. This hampers and at its extreme paralyses the thinking and operational ability of individuals and even whole organisations. The adoption of information is as slow as ever. People do not have the level of literacy they are assumed to have. This stormy surface impairs the understanding of total concepts and the development of new information.

Understanding of information and messages is also hampered by the internal 'multiculture' of organisations created not just by different nationalities and languages but also by different age groups and different educational and vocational backgrounds. In the work environment, differing kinds of training and vocational backgrounds can prove greater obstacles than that of differing mother tongues. There are differences in the way people of different age groups process information. A lot of attention has to be paid to understanding the exchange of information and communication in a work environment that incorporates differing kinds of people. The Corporate Literacy level of this kind of an organisation has to be versatile but inevitably, makes dealing with matters more complex.

The bubble of the new economics at the turn of the twenty-first century was an example of what will happen when action is taken based purely on fast surface information. The companies creating new media believed and persuaded others of the accuracy of their belief that electronic trading and business was something completely new with no connection to the past. When even the basics in trading and business were not taken into consideration it was obvious to anybody with even slight experience in these fields that the companies could not succeed on this basis. Knowledge born of experience was not utilised in this atmosphere of huge enthusiasm.

Internet companies made their first moves based on inadequate logistics and customer knowledge. Products were made available on the Internet without considering how the customers could find and buy them. It was imagined that new technology and visual representation would be sufficient. From a customer point of view, this proved blatantly unsatisfactory. Internet trading, where it was impossible to buy even when desperate to buy, was doomed to failure. The venture was based on insufficient information as regards the trade itself, the customers and their needs. In many cases the funding capital of these companies was not the obstacle. They were given so much risk funding capital that it could have been used to buy knowledge and experience.

Both the Internet companies and their financiers possessed a narrow surface level literacy. Forecasts for the future were being read selectively, gleaned from the surface of the news flow while slow development processes were not taken into consideration. Once the dot.com surface layer disappeared, solid business operations have slowly risen from underneath, which more slowly but greater surety, utilise technology and information networks in their operations.

## History, current situation and future

The information strategy must provide an assertion as to which issues require a literacy of the history, the current situation, the future or all of these and how the literacy requirements are emphasised.

| Figure 2.2 | Surface information – deep information and information strategy |

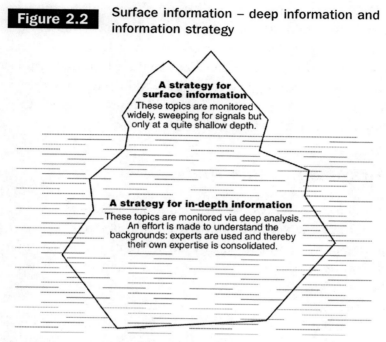

The previous example relating to the Internet bubble also applies here. The Internet companies and their investors read only information relating to the future while side-stepping the history, i.e. what were the requirements for traditional trading and business. The new phenomena creating great expectations focused all the attention forward. On the other hand, when these kinds of expectations collapse, the tendency is to again hang on to the past, with the result that a careful analysis as regards the current situation is not undertaken and the weak signals revealing the changes regarding the future are ignored. For example, Internet business operations as well as many other activities using information networks have proceeded in spite of the bursting of the bubble of the new economics, however, not with the speed predicted when expectations were at their peak.

It is difficult to get an idea about the current situation while caught up in the midst of change in a complex environment. By the time there is some understanding of initial changes, many of the issues have altered and there has been a move to the next stage. All three time dimensions have to be continuously observed within the organisation and literacy needs to be developed within a context that takes account of the past, the present and the future.

## *Away from insular thinking*

When information is mainly sited in information networks and when the starting point is that the organisation does not employ a limited, closed system but rather, a changing formation of people, their networks and contacts, the division between internal and external information and knowledge of the organisation is theoretical and artificial.

From the perspective of Corporate Literacy, entirely internal organisational information and knowledge doesn't exist. Each individual continuously receives information from outside. This information is connected and mixed continuously with his/her previous knowledge. This relates to both printed and electronic information, to information received from other people and from observation of the environment. The information of an individual is continuously revised within his/her activities and always has a context. Only if trapped in a dark, enclosed space, where she/he has no connection to other people and the outside world does an individual function entirely based on internal knowledge. Equally, thoughts of the internal information of an organisation or society are absurd in a digital networked environment unless we are talking about a prison camp with no access to the external world.

Corporate Literacy is the skill to read information flows, then to connect and create something new from them. There is no static mode. Michael Koenig sees as the next stage of the Knowledge Management approach as paying keen attention to the external information and knowledge. Until now, the overwhelming emphasis of Knowledge Management to date has been to mobilise and make accessible the organisation's information and knowledge. The focus has been inside the organisation.

There is also a risk in the intranets of organisations of a concentration merely on the customary information resources while giving less consideration to the external information flows. Construction of extranets has been much slower indeed. The fears about spreading information to competitors and the risks connected with information security have had an effect on this. The insularity of organisations is, however, often displayed on their Internet pages in the manner they offer information about themselves. Language often utilises the jargon of the organisation itself or of its operational field and information is organised from the perspective of the organisation. The primary position is held by the organisations that have been able to develop their web pages to be more variable and open in order also to extend across the outside world and its concomitant information resources and flows.

Companies and public administrations have to develop their externally targeted literacy in order to understand the expectations required of them as regards their customers desires and needs. In a networked environment the customers have access to worldwide information resources and the possibility to compare services, products and various information sources. A self-centred, closed organisation is not able to compete in this environment.

Insular thinking in a style of 'If only Texas Instruments knew what Texas Instruments knew' will not lead anywhere. Innovations are not created in a confined environment. A large part of the key information needed for critical decisions lies outside of the company so the information systems have to provide links to the outside world. New ideas normally come from outside, from another field and/or from unexpected connections arising as a result of several factors. Usability, meaning and the value of information is decided by its proportion in relation to other information and knowledge.

The question is what touches us, that is, what is important to use in respect of the situation and/or task relative to the economic, political, geographical and cultural environments as well as what information we select to monitor based upon these. There are many selective possibilities that may lead us to very different interpretations, decisions and solutions.

Finally we must ask the following: Does an organisation act dynamically, using all its senses or does it work mechanistically, using accustomed information channels? Is the organisation mechanistic and bureaucratic as are organisations belonging to an industrial society or dynamic, flexible and creative as are the organisations belonging to a network society?

## *Information strategy is executed by people*

Information strategy, as with the adoption of all strategies through the practices within the organisation, requires management level understanding of staff level literacy. Information strategy is not executed on paper but through the activities of people. This kind of processing requires continuous justification and takes place in people's work, discussions and interaction. Discussions can be activated via electronic and telecommunication equipment but there is also a requirement for direct meetings and physical presence.

Information loading causes a lot of insecurity in people. It can be alleviated through regular meetings and consultations where the insecurities can be expressed and where it is possible to discuss openly both problems and possible solutions. It is important to be aware of any ignorance, insecurity or less than comprehensive skills and task completion. People can only alleviate insecurities through genuinely open meetings where insecurities and problems can be expressed frankly and participants listen to one another. Face-to-face meetings generate abundant information flows among participating individuals. When fear and tensions can be dissipated via face-to-face meetings everyone's energy is boosted, which can then be redirected to each individual's own work. This allows for a more realistic view of the current situation and thereby leads to a greater clarification of the goals that need to be attained. What is important is confidence in mutual support. The creation and success of this method of operation requires maturity, effective social skills and significant commitment.

# How does an organisation read its environment

An organisation obtains information from its environment by observing, listening, clarifying, researching, collecting signals and analysing long chain processes and then organises the information required before making it available for use via networks and support services. Comprehensive Literacy is founded on the identification and use of all its senses. One of the great illusions of today, which also affects high-level decision-makers and managers, is that everybody can easily access any required external information via Google. This falsely leads to the company believing its own information resources and Google are sufficient, as everybody can obtain something from Google by typing in just a couple of words. When this view holds sway, the informational development of companies and society is brought to a halt.

In 2005 Shell, wanting to obtain an in-depth understanding about its operational environment, the state of the world and future perspectives, prepared an extensive globalisation report. Shell invited a large group of experts it considered to be the best and requested from them a research report relating to the subject. Shell's extensive, multidisciplined report is an example of the formation of in-depth information, but is also an example of a slow process. Long-term processes and deep currents are observed this way and their effects on the future are predicted. Equivalent reports are occasionally undertaken for use by companies and decision-makers in society. An analytical and in-depth, one-off inspection is useful and important, but still not sufficient.

Though high-level decision-makers have all possible information channels, resources and networks at their disposal, they live an existence so remote from the rest of society, in their black limousines, attending banquets and fetes peopled by similarly powerful individuals, that by the time they become aware of a crucial gap in their information concerning their working population or the operational environment of their company, it is too late. However, the situation has already become clear to ordinary citizens. When the environment is rapidly changing and insecure, the condition of the operational environment should be continuously observed and monitored using all the sensors and radars of the organisation and the findings should be collected, documented and analysed.

I was involved in analysing the organisational and developmental needs of the information services of a Finnish ministry at the beginning of the 1990s. I interviewed staff, officials and management of the ministry concerned and one among them was an official preparing a new law for the organisation of regional administration. After a lengthy discussion, this very experienced lawyer suddenly said: 'How would it be possible to get information about the state of society?' I was taken aback. How can a high-level official working in the public administration of a democratic county, with a legal background stretching back over decades and with access to all the ministerial expertise and information resources ask such a question?

Finland at that time was in the initial grip of a recession, which became unexpectedly serious. Companies went bankrupt and unemployment was increasing rapidly. The changes in these circumstances were both brutal and abrupt. It was widely debated at a national level but the overwhelming experience was a harsh one, particularly for entrepreneurs and for those who became suddenly unemployed. Most people had family members or acquaintances that were suddenly in financial difficulties. I was of the opinion that there was nothing unclear about the condition of the society. I felt that my role as an information specialist and professional interviewer was being pushed to the limits of tolerance. Did he really not understand the condition of the society? I was thinking to myself that all that he needed was to travel on the underground or visit the nearest pub and listen to the people.

These questions stayed with me. Now and then a management group or a manager gets the idea that we should find out exactly what is the state of the society, the nation state or the globe. This can be undertaken and at its best it will produce an excellent cross-sectional view of the situation. However, this kind of a procedure is not sufficient as a response to the needs of an organisation operating in the modern world, nor of an administrative unit nor of company management and its operations. Once the results are obtained from this kind of a procedure, it is often too late. The companies and public administration have to be constantly alert to the operational environment and they have to have the methods to obtain information from it from different perspectives. Information monitoring and analysis have to be continuous. We also need methods to obtain collected and analysed information fast in changing circumstances.

The above example also shows that the normal information monitoring methods of an organisation do not necessarily reach the top management or these methods themselves do not respond to their needs. It may be normal practice for decision-makers to rely on sources and networks that are either too, or entirely inappropriate, when searching information. A high-level example of the failure of monitoring through a reliance upon inaccurate sources was the assertion made first by President George Bush, soon after seconded by the UK Prime Minister Tony Blair, stating Iraq had access to weapons of mass destruction. This led to a long warring path.

The construction of a monitoring apparatus over an operational environment is a demanding task. It has to resolve which issues are to be monitored, which channels used and who is to be listened to. Eclecticism has to be the order of the day in terms of the selection of the targets for continuous monitoring. As well as simply listening to what ordinary people have to say, targets of continuous monitoring should include the media, research results, literature, films, the opinions of the rural and urban population, of immigrants, of the unemployed, and of representatives of minorities, not to mention the prevailing opinion in the suburbs and the rest of the whole wide world. The issues have to be widely observed and reaction has to be aimed at important issues, then these have to be given resources and the focus has to be on success in these areas or on the correction of possible problems in these areas.

The society or organisation need not be large or wealthy to develop this kind of environmental monitoring and procedure. If a small organisation suffers from a severe social or health problem and there is a common desire to correct it (AIDS, tuberculosis, adult diabetes, drugs, criminality), the literacy of the organisation can be targeted and focused on this issue (via libraries, schools, social and health authorities, local media, politicians, also possibly via company services and company product development). To correct these kinds of matters the literacy of individuals is not sufficient in and of itself. Using the complementary skills (information attainment and transmission skills, information technical skills, specialist knowledge) of the people belonging to the organisation it is possible to utilise the abundant information resources available via information networks and people networks worldwide. It is extremely important to edit the information prior to distribution, so that it can be understood and utilised by the members of the organisation. Using visual presentations it is possible to raise the information level of an organisation, even in one that may include a number of illiterate people. Shared goals and a common will are essential requirements if changes are to be implemented with regard to the application of information.

## Senses for selecting information

It is more important to make conscious value judgements of what is important than it is to monitor as much information as possible. What is the focus? Which markets should the focus be directed toward? Who are the customers? What is the current operational environment and what is the desired operational environment? Why? What lies ahead?

What makes the selection of information difficult in an insecure environment is the fact that we can never be certain which information may become significant as regards our operations and furthermore, what kind of information is it that future plans should be based upon. It is possible that a product development or a technical innovation from an entirely different operational field may result in the launching of a product that makes the companies major product redundant. It is possible that we have plans for the society, for building schools and hospitals, entirely unaware of the gathering clouds of war crowding the horizon, a war, which like all wars, will sate its appetite for destruction through the demolition of all development and construction work. However, before one gives in to bleak futility, it must be said, there are always advance signals. Therefore, it is crucial that the selected mode of monitoring is both flexible and adaptable. By joining together different kinds of information fragments and by monitoring long-term processes an opinion can be formed about what may lie ahead. Information monitoring has to be simultaneously systematic and eclectic and it should always leave channels open to the influx of new and surprising elements.

With my mind's eye I visualise the organisation of an information society as an amoeba-like creature that explores its environment multidirectionally, receives messages via moving, information sensitive tentacles, reacts, shifts, alters shape based on the messages received, and even temporarily joins with other creatures, only to separate again, itself transformed. To foster effective selection of information an organisation needs the senses, instinct and responsiveness required to rationalise between conflicting messages.

## Reading different fields and cultures

Development of literacy relating to different fields and different cultures is necessary in a networked and multiskilled workplace. The languages used by different professions are also increasingly specific, which makes cooperation more difficult even within the organisations. Based on Fruchter and Emery (1999) learning of multifield co-operative behaviour can be divided into four stages: (1) islands of knowledge; (2) awareness; (3) appreciation; and (4) understanding.

Young people who have just completed their studies often know their own field and its most recent information but have hardly any experience with regard to other fields. They are islands of knowledge. The first step for learning multifield cooperation is the development of an awareness relating to the goals and restrictions of other fields. The next stage is achievable once an effort is made to round up concepts relating to other fields, a desire to understand and support the goals of the other field is fostered and an ability to ask the right questions is developed. This will, at the same time, develop an appreciation for the work of professional colleagues from other fields. Good progress has been made in learning multifield cooperation once the conceptual understanding relating to the other fields has been achieved. It is then possible to negotiate and take a proactive approach when entering into discussion with representatives of other fields. It also allows for the possibility of offering one's own contribution and expertise without the need for it to be requested. At this stage it is possible to meet with the representative of a different field using his/her language. These learning stages are completed through cross-learning between representatives of professional, organisational and national cultures.

## Development of information and Knowledge Management within organisations

Information Resource Management introduced by Woody Horton in the 1980s opened a view to the information resources of the whole organisation. The role of information as a resource was understood and the aim was to manage and utilise the information resources of the whole organisation. At its best, attention was paid to numerical, text and visual information, information system's data, printed and human information sources. The Information Resources Management approach expanded understanding of the role of the information services to cover the different types of information resources of the whole organisation. In practice, the comprehensive view concerning information resources has been realised in the fact that there has been an aim to stretch the information systems to cover the entire informational content of an organisation. Comprehensive and integrated management of documents and contents has, however, progressed very slowly in comparison with the speed of technical development.

Consultation companies introduced the Knowledge Management approach to organisations simultaneously, with the breakthrough of the Internet.

The exciting simultaneous components were on the one hand different approaches to Knowledge Management, for example, the Knowledge Management cycle by Nonaka and Takeuchi (1995), which tied tacit knowledge to the formation of the organisational knowledge, and on the other hand, the possibilities opened up by information technology. Both the people emphasising skills and information technology and companies providing development in respect of Knowledge Management, were viewed as exciting. These matters were not at that time particularly connected with the search and organisation of documented information. Knowledge Management was mainly shaped according to how the leading international consultants introduced it into the companies, rather than it taking shape based on the development needs of the organisations. Knowledge Management can be criticised in that it maintained the debate between management, consultants and other enthusiastic parties but failed to detect an echo within the reality of the daily regimen within organisations. When finding information still appeared to be difficult with the expansion of the Internet, company intranets and extranets the suppliers of the systems and the information technology specialists invented magic terms such as meta-data, taxonomy and content management. These words gained power only after they passed into the lingua franca of the information technology developers.

The time is now ripe to combine different approaches and thereby create a synthesis. This requires cooperation from all of the parties working with information and knowledge within an organisation as well as identification of, and recognition for, the skills of each special field.

Creation of every good product and service yields a plethora of information associated with the execution of the idea, the production process, customers, customer needs and the method of distribution. Information intensity in products has increased, the markets have expanded and the competition hardened while production processes and customer needs have become more complex.

Company information management follows the changes in information concepts and technology and the wider social and economic development. The changes can be traced retrospectively moving from the industrial society through to the service society and up to the information society. Besides product development and economic information there is also a need to systematically attain, monitor and organise information relating to customers and the wider operational environment and the changes it undergoes. The concept of information has, in addition to documented number and text information, been expanded, to recognise the role of tacit knowledge and the knowledge of experience. The concept relating to knowledge which has been deconstructed as is the fashion with post-modernity is continuously changing and fairly hazy. Instead of historical knowledge the search is for signals and an understanding of the future; an understanding of something of what does not exist yet. There is a desire for new knowledge and innovation.

What then is the level of corporate information management and literacy? Although, in theory, it should be more than the sum of its parts, in reality it may in fact be less than the sum of its parts in many organisations. Such organisations lack awareness with regard to the organisations senses and tentacles, nor can they combine their internal resources. Tacit knowledge and hidden skills are not revealed. Companies, public administration units and organisations have become systems that suppress people instead of encouraging them to combine their strengths.

## *What next?*

Michael E. D. Koenig has outlined the development curve of Knowledge Management by separating three stages in which, for the present at least, the following characteristics are typical (Koenig 2005):

- Stage 1: Internet and intellectual capital
  - Information technology
  - Intellectual capital
  - The Internet (intranets, extranets, etc.)
  - Key phrases: 'best practices', later replaces by the more politic 'lessons learned'
- Stage 2: Human and cultural dimensions, human relations
  - Communities of practice
  - Organisational culture
  - The Learning Organisation and
  - Tacit Knowledge incorporated into Knowledge Management
  - Key phrase: 'communities of practice'
- Stage 3: Content and retrieval
  - Structuring content and assigning descriptors (index terms)
  - Key phrases: content management and taxonomies.

Koenig (2005) sees that the fourth stage as shaping and believes that the defining characteristic of that stage is an awareness of the importance of the external information and knowledge of the organisation. The next stage includes a new kind of information architecture design, i.e. structures for the information flows based on information strategy. I would like to add Corporate Literacy as the fifth stage.

## Finding new ways to organise and present information: designing new information architecture

We know, based on common experience and the calculations carried out by Berkeley University that information grows exponentially (Lyman and Varian 2003). Different cultures, professional fields, languages, experts, citizens, practices and ways of presentation come together on the Internet. The Internet is a genuine Tower of Babel. Exponential growth almost inevitably, means uncontrollable growth. Bacteria, viruses and cancer cells grow exponentially. The quality of Internet content varies from the reporting of scientific results to largely superficial trivia, from criminal material to legal information, from pornography to the arts. It is all there in parallel coexistence, occupying the same cyberspace, while our current search engines struggle to provide any coherent, meaningful differentiation. They only recognise character strings. Ironically, as search engines have become more efficient at recognising character strings, the quality of the search results has become worse. Better organisation of information is needed but how can it be achieved?

Internet sites proliferate and link to one another like urban slums. The self-help drive behind the construction of slums has its own visual richness, which also reflects human creativity even in the midst of appalling conditions. The tourists romanticise slums as examples of the exotic and the picturesque; however, those living in slums can only dream about escaping from them. Efforts are also directed to reconstruct and renew the slums. Some of the slums have even been totally destroyed via explosive demolition.

However, the human living environment should be built upon a different basis. The same applies to the information environment – both physical and virtual. We shouldn't fall into the trap of thinking that if we allow the information environment to be self-directing we will be able to develop our literacy and thus make sense of the ever-expanding, miscellaneous information mass. Improvement of information management requires a lot of energy, restructuring and the renewal of current systems. Furthermore, incorrect, outdated and unnecessary information should be regularly destroyed. In addition to the improvement in literacy the information environment itself should be improved.

Corporate Literacy includes the ability to communicate and to set one's own information resources for use by others, while simultaneously taking into consideration future needs. No information system should be designed without taking into consideration communicative factors, which individuals or groups may require information and how the information can be distributed and utilised. A literate organisation does not store information but organises it so that it is easily accessible for various purposes. Corporate Literacy means having the skill to analyse and organise one's own information resources qualitatively and into a usable form. This requires a new kind of awareness and responsibility in respect of the producer of information.

Current methods to organise information resources as well as the usability of the information require critical inspection. Typically information resources are organised egocentrically from the perspective of the organisation. Often for an acute, short-term need and using the organisation's own jargon and classifications, starting from the perspective of the producer and paying little attention to other information users nor future requirements. This is reflected in the Internet, extranet and intranet services, where the different users are in immediate contact with the organisation's information supply. In a networking society information, right from the beginning of the process, should be produced in a manner that considers other parties information needs, different individual user needs, as well as allowing for multipurpose linking of apparently disparate information.

By convention, information architecture has been considered merely an underlying characteristic of web page design characteristic. However, it underlies all information systems, information environments, not to mention the organisation as a whole. Information architecture forms the structures underpinning information flows. Structures create order. They set information in an order of importance facilitating the implementation of conscious or non-conscious strategy. Structures open and close information flows, make some of them visible and hide others. Information architecture is also an indication of networks where the organisation is participating. Information architecture is based on literacy of the organisation. A literate organisation is aware of its information architecture, assesses its structures and aims to keep information channels open and flexibly renewable.

The following points have to be taken into consideration when assessing information architecture structures and information flows:

- What information fields the information flows cover?

- Who or which parties produce the information used?

- Which networks are behind the information architecture?

- Have the required information types and information formats been taken into consideration?

- Is there any information relating to the past, the present or the future?

- Has the contrast between rapidly changing 'surface information' and slow process 'deep information' been taken into consideration?

It is important to identify which information flows are not covered by the architecture. Furthermore, the updating of information and possibilities for the entry of new information also need to be considered.

The organisation supports the literacy of its staff and customers by analysing and organising its information resources into easily usable formats. In the same way as organisations organise their staff work facilities, the organisations have to pay attention to the information space of their staff and its information architecture, as well as the physical and virtual net space. For an organisation to succeed in its tasks, it is important to create information spaces where, in the words by Dr Kiti Müller (2003) 'the brains are feeling well'. This is an ergonomic issue promoting work productivity but is also a critical factor in the reduction of risks and human error. There is a big challenge in the relationship between individual and group organisational information spaces. What is individual and what is shared? How much individual freedom can be ceded without preventing shared accessibility? How many general regulations can be set without restricting radical thinking and fresh innovation?

Advanced and comprehensive Corporate Literacy requires a new kind of way to organise its Knowledge and Knowledge Space both in the physical and virtual worlds. This assumes a new kind of architecture, moving the design of the Knowledge Systems and Internet Services on to a new stage. It is not sufficient that knowledge/data are accessible via retrieval from whatever the chosen method of storage. Based on research on the use of information it is now well known that users apply the principle of minimum effort and are satisfied with minimal return. In the physical environment information is searched for usually, within a distance of no more than a couple of metres, while similarly, in the virtual environment a search generally constitutes no more than a couple of search words and a minimum amount of clicks. Users have neither the time nor inclination to pursue lengthy searches to meet the continuous demand for current, up to date information, stored in the depths of the system. Knowledge has to be unambiguously present, within visual 'reach' and must be in both an easily readable and usable form.

The visibility created by information architecture does not mean that the information used would be superficial as regards its content. The contents of advanced information architecture are continuously assessed, developed and kept updated. Information from the deep networks and from alternative, also conflicting information sources is lifted to the near environment and to the 'surface'. Taking care of the versatility of the information content and its visibility is indeed a challenging task. Solid cooperation by information architects, by information specialists and by the parties requiring information and by the experts is required here. Here also a stand should be taken as regards what is important and it needs an ability to assess the contents and reliability and coverage of the sources.

Information architecture is a visible part of Corporate Literacy. Corporate Literacy shifts the emphasis to information architecture content, rather than the creation of the 'technical' organisation and usability, as has been the norm until now. Information architecture creates a window from which it is possible to gaze upon the outside world or alternatively, into the organisation itself.

## *Development of information environment: information ecology*

In the same way as the architecture of a building or a city is always planned within the context of some pre-existing natural or built environment, the information architecture is always created into some existing information environment – information ecology (Nardi and O'Day 1999). It includes various information resources representing different formats, information technology, net connections and their users, the physical environment, operational skills, practices and values, i.e. information culture. A networked information environment is simultaneously, global and local. The global information environment can be accessed via networked connections. Localised information materials, people and their information culture, form the local context. Localised information is also becoming a ubiquitous presence in all information, meaning that information used globally will always have a local and regional dimension. We are approaching a time when accurate up-to-date information can be searched in connection with any physical location.

The information environment is utilised as per the actual situation or task. A school, a hospital, a company, a nursing home, a residential area, each have their own information ecology. Equally, so does an international company and its subsidiary. Different kinds of user environments can generate their own unique view of their technology, information resources and information usage. Furthermore, people, their knowledge and skills constitute an integral part of information ecology.

Therefore, information ecology is a complex system of various parts and their relationships to one another. The different parts have an effect on each other and cause changes via each other throughout the whole system. This kind of a system, consisting of people, their habits, their equipment and informational content, is complex, as is nature's ecology but aims to respond to local needs. Richness and diversity are typical characteristics of this kind of entity.

Before starting to plan the information architecture of an organisation, the wider information environment and its information ecology need to be studied. A varied methodology should be employed in carrying out this task: previous analyses; studies and other literary sources; interviews and surveys; as well as observations concerning people's working methods and information search, retrieval and utilisation behaviour. The broader the entity constituting the target for information planning, the more thoroughly the information environment has to be studied and the more complex the methodology is required to be. Analysis of the Information environment should be approached in the same fashion as ethnographers approach the analysis of a different culture. Outlining the information environment and developing an understanding of the information ecology are an integral part of Corporate Literacy.

Information architecture provides space and context with regard to information. Comprehensive Corporate Literacy takes into consideration information and knowledge formats, as well as other aspects that are important from the perspective of the operation of the organisation. It is not essential for information to be external or internal. Both are required and they cannot be fully separated. It is essential to identify information that exists in different formats and to organise information and knowledge flows into good information architecture (which involves content management and the meta-layer providing the relative taxonomic and meta-information) and the skills, required to utilise this environment based on the selected strategy.

Information ecology offers an organisation with the resources to attain, refine, edit and transfer information while interacting with customers, partners and society as a whole. As information and knowledge are the raw materials of an organisation, the organisation has to design and construct its own information architecture in a manner that provides tangible bridges to information resources an easily usable format suitable for the particular demands of a given situation. The traditional target of information services being able to offer the right information, at the right time, to the right place is still relevant and provides an appropriate target for information architecture.

## User friendliness: customer's literacy

The World Wide Web and its browser technologies currently provide a user interface offering access to almost all information and in almost every possible format (text, video, audio, etc.), via an open Internet, the intranets of organisations, as well as extranets between organisations. The user has greater choice and more control than is the case with any other existing media. The user doesn't have to watch or listen to the programme from beginning to end; neither is he/she dependent on the content of a single book but can change 'the books' and pages as he/she pleases. At the same time he/she also has a bigger workload than in any other media as a result of having to sift through mountains of information and make snap decisions over which information to collect or discard. The task of the information architecture is to lighten this load by offering as logical, understandable and pleasant information environment as possible. Thus, in order to reduce this workload right from the very start, design has to be based on the needs of the user.

Owing to the fact that the workload rests heaviest upon the user, the user's needs, operating environment and function have to be identified in the planning of the information architecture in greater depth than when producing traditional information products for printed or electronic communication equipment. A target group analysis is not sufficient. Even the target group concept reflects the views of customers and users as the views of passive targets. In constructing information networks we are dealing with active and independent parties, not targets to be controlled from the outside.

We are talking about understanding the needs of the customer. User friendliness means that the perspective of a customer is always taken into consideration at all the stages of all systematic methods:

- The customer groups are identified (we know who we are talking to and why).

- Customer groups are known (information is obtained from them using different methods).

- The viewpoint of the customer, the operational situation, the operational environment and skills are taken into consideration in the service provided and the implementation of that service

- The usability perspectives are taken into consideration in planning and testing.

- Feedback is obtained and the service is improved based on this.

Grouping, identification and the development of a knowledge base about customers are complex issues. People function in different roles as customers, users, consumers and citizens. They represent different cultures and language areas. One person can have many roles. It is important to know the demographic characteristics (age, gender, language, culture) relating to an eclectic customer base but it is not enough in and of itself. Information is required about their needs, wishes, expectations, situational context, as well as to what information and communication technology they have access to. The knowledge base should include an assessment of their information and network literacy levels. Across the Internet, people directly enter public (and sometimes private) spaces without anyone acting as an intermediary or guide. Furthermore, they use routes of their own choosing and come and go as they please. It is important to get to know them in a fashion that mirrors the way people get to know one another in small rural communities. It is important to obtain information about the person in general, about the way the person learns, about the changes the ageing process age might bring, as well as about the person's living conditions. An information architect designing information environments has to know the people who will inhabit that environment in much the same way as a building architect has to know the people who will inhabit the building he/she is designing.

## Climbing the steps toward the utilisation of information

Utilisation of information cannot be evaluated step by step. I have asked my clients to evaluate the utilisation of the information of their organisations or Internet services by going through the information utilisation steps from the point of view of the users: access, usability, readability, intelligibility, reliability and meaning. Often the users have already stopped at the first step, i.e. at the entry to information. This was a surprise, for example, for a music

**Figure 2.3** Information utilisation steps

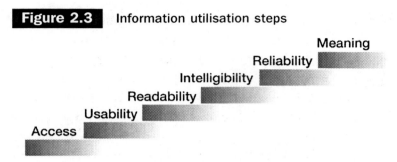

college, aiming to offer the students via the Internet as much information as possible. It was found that many of these students didn't have access to the Internet at home. The computer was not their main instrument. Neither did the college itself have a sufficient number of computers and connections at the disposal of its students.

When access has been arranged for all user groups, the usability of the information has to be evaluated: how easy is the information system to use and learn. Accessibility, readability and intelligibility of the information have to be evaluated. Care as regards the reliability of the information is important right from the beginning as the errors in a digital environment increase exponentially at tremendous speed and are difficult to trace and correct.

Information should be up-to-date and visible at all times in the relevant locations where it is required. Information needs to be accessible for old and young. It should be available to all parties needing it, in all required languages and of course, it must be readable and intelligible. It is necessary to climb to the top step of utilisation in order to evaluate the most important thing, i.e. the meaning of information. These steps should also be seen from the perspective of enterprise usability.

## Visibility of information: presentation of information

Success in the design of the visibility of information is the key to comprehensive access. A similar visibility is the goal in the design of department stores. All the products have to be accessible according to the logic of the customer and they have to be visible. There also has to be the possibility of discovering information when the customer doesn't know how to search for it. Transportation logistics, routes, instructions and product descriptions have to be planned to facilitate high-level display and visibility of appropriate information. There should always be access to personal advice, i.e. an information point is required. Information planners find it useful to study the best-planned department stores and traffic systems.

Corporate Literacy covers the management of all of the information life cycle, as well as an ability to edit and package the information into a usable form. This means that information is packaged in a form appropriate to the situation and context. If there is a need to transmit medical information to a rural village, it is not sufficient that the information should exist on one of the Internet's medical sites as an English language research report. When transmitting information to a certain local society, the language of that community has to be used. The language has to be understandable and when transmitting the information the channels and equipment used by the parties receiving it have to be used. If information has to be transmitted to a certain professional group, it makes sense to use the specific terminology of said group or a generally understood language. In order to have a tangible effect on operations in the utilisation of information, there has to be significant investment into the presentation and packaging of information.

## *Memory and ability of an organisation to look into the future*

It has been suggested that evolution has promoted a rather poor memory faculty in humans, as regards small details, to facilitate, even force the utilisation of the human capacities for thinking, classification of phenomena and instinctive pursuit of symmetry. An individual who has developed the ability of classification and conceptualisation is able, based on a very small amount of information, to make useful hypotheses that could not otherwise be developed via individual observation alone. A bad memory as regards the past provides space and ability to see into the future.

If this analogy is also applied to an organisation there should be a freeing up of space and a strengthening of the ability to analyse matters and to look to the future instead of operating solely on the basis of a weak memory. It is known that in many organisations the search for information based upon the combination of a poor memory and a generally weak organisation wastes approximately one-third of total working time. If greater productivity is the goal, then this time could be reclaimed through improvements in the visibility and availability of information. Therefore the information architecture should be arranged so that finding information is not based on the fragile human memory, but instead makes information easily observable and quickly accessible via the literacy of the people working within the organisation. This requires improvements in the 'visibility' of the information and the possibility of finding the information so that any required information is accessible anywhere at any time. Visibility is required as otherwise we will not know what information is available for use.

# Empowering and sharing as key words

Literacy is a tool for **empowering**. Throughout history the basic literacy has opened possibilities for economic and social progress, such as the growing influence of the working class, women and other previously marginalised sections of populations. Empowering people to act and participate effectively in their own work, communities, society (both local and national), as well as to address global questions, is extremely important. Comprehensive Information Literacy and communication are necessary tools for people, companies and communities. They facilitate inclusion. Information and communication technology increases the possibilities of activity for people with learning difficulties, older people and for people alienated or excluded somehow from others. Furthermore, small and start-up enterprises benefit from this irrespective of where they choose to operate. Information networks provide possibilities for learning, for attainment of information and for participation. In addition to the computer and network connections everyone needs literacy skills to be able to benefit fully from these possibilities. However, technologies, skills and requirements for empowerment are unfairly distributed between countries and continents and indeed, within countries, regions and communities.

Corporate Literacy of an organisation is constructed based upon the literacy skills of its members and their interconnectivity. Empowerment of these people means empowerment of the organisation. Exclusion of these same people, as a consequence of insufficient literacy skills, is a huge hindrance to the development of companies and society as a whole.

It is important to foster and support people's participation in the production of contents, net communication, and exerting an influence over their own work environment. In studies relating to the use of the Internet by young people, for example, this leaving of one's own, personalised trail, has been found to be of very great significance. The feeling of empowerment and participation is strengthened by the fact that one's own activities leave a visible track.

The method required to avoid excluding people is sharing. Among citizens and consumers there has been a continuous, ongoing development of activities for which the open sharing of information and communality is typical. Examples of this include Open Source Community and Open Access Movement promoting fast accessibility and transmission of information of research publications by research societies. A new and surprising phenomenon is the Internet's open encyclopaedia, Wikipedia, which can be edited by anyone. These phenomena have been self-directing and the associated commitment and enthusiasm has been surprising. How many people would have believed that an encyclopaedia, maintained in such a full and open fashion across the Internet, could contain reliable information? Yet the quality of Wikipedia remains high in many areas due to the expertise and activities of thousands of people who monitor it voluntarily.

One of the most recent phenomena is folksonomy, which appeared during 2005 in Internet blogs and discussions. According to Wikipedia, folksonomy, a portmanteau word combining 'folk' and 'taxonomy' refers to the collaborative but unsophisticated way in which information is being categorised on the web. Instead of using a centralised form of classification, users are encouraged to assign freely chosen keywords (called tags) to pieces of information or data, a process known as tagging. Examples of web services that use tagging include those designed to allow users to publish and share photographs (http://www.flickr.com) and bookmarks (http://del.icio.us). (See also http://en.wikipedia.org/wiki/Folksonomy)

There is a long history in terms of the efforts that have been made to find a universal way to classify information and libraries, through international cooperation, have made highly significant progress in the development of common classifications. On the other hand, different fields of science and different organisational cultures have their own classification practices and regulations. Companies have tried to organise their own information using taxonomies of their own. Common to the various classifications and terminologies is the fact that information professionals have until now, been responsible for the drafting and often, application of them.

It is important that information professionals share their knowledge, accumulated as a result of their own attainment, evaluation and meta-knowledge, with others working within the organisation. The burden for the search of information within the Internet falls on the so-called end-users themselves, while the actual information search services offered by library and information services are disappearing. However, finding information, even from the Internet, is not simple. The form of the search, planning of the search strategy, and use of the various search engines and directories requires knowledge that the information specialists can teach as trainers, advisers and support groups to the end-users. The Internet environment also requires guidance and instruction about these matters. The information specialists play an important part as designers of the information architecture of the Internet services and as developers of such Internet-based learning environments in which the tools for information search and networked information resources are used effectively.

Meta-information enables wide distribution and connection of information for different purposes. An important area for the sharing of information is the sharing of knowledge connected with meta-data. Traditionally, the information specialists and libraries upheld this skill. When the burden of finding the information falls on the end-user, the accessibility of the information is mainly the responsibility of the original provider. The aim is that the majority of meta-data would be saved automatically, but not everything can be automated. The creator of the document, who is familiar with the content of the document, should in the first place give a name, a title and other meta-information describing it clearly, making it accessible to searches employing key words, information relating to the creator and date, etc. Ordinary authors, among whom I would include specialists representing different fields, however, still do not, while writing, consider how different people will approach their writing, how they will search for it and what kind of keywords they will use. The creator of the document may also be ignorant as to what future perspective the document will searched from. Who is the best describer of information: the information producer, the publisher, the supplier, the information specialist, or the user of the information? Perhaps, in addition to automation, contributions from all of them are required, which in reality means that to produce and publish information is a communal activity. In that case, we need comprehensive understanding of what is the role of meta-data from the perspective of accessibility of information.

The spreading of folksonomy may revolutionise the classification and the traditional practices and roles of description relating to information. This phenomenon is also connected with daily and easily learnt terminology: we talk about tags, bundles and tag clouds instead of keywords, categories and thesaurus.

Methods for application of existing equivalent ways to organise and share information should also be searched by organisations, for example, the management of intranets and documents. A lot of power, often expertise power, is connected with information classification and organisation. Based on classification, information can be made visible or remain hidden. folksonomy represents a bottom-up approach to the organisation of information.

These phenomena are interesting from the point of view of companies and public administration. Is it possible to apply the same innovative operational models to them that people have learnt to use in the open Internet? Both of the keywords, empowering and sharing, combined with information and Corporate Literacy are revolutionary as regards the perspective of the operations of organisations. At the same time they clash with the hierarchical structures of organisations and old ways of operating. Furthermore, copyrights can create an obstruction to the distribution of information. Power structures, competition between companies, trading associations and individuals, as well as egocentricity, negate empowerment and open distribution of information and may even create a conflict. Nor do insecure and stressful working conditions provide the motivation to operate positively and socially.

Management of an exponentially expanding information mountain, browsing, analysing and interpreting of essential information is so demanding that the only possible way to act is through collaboration between as many parties as possible, sharing of information as a part of information culture. This sharing has to include great responsibility. We all know of people who 'openly' share their email with anybody without filtering and interpreting the various documents received by them. The receiver may, for a while at least, try to read these with interest until he/she decides they will no longer put up with being a refuse pit where masses of non-sorted informational rubbish is delivered.

This does not constitute sharing of information but rather an irresponsible spreading and increasing of information pollution.

Transparency in the development of Corporate Literacy requires that all the parties belonging to the organisation actively share their information and are able to do so via channels specially created to facilitate this. It is not possible obtain information and thereby participate in wider knowledge building if people are not willing to share information. Some of the developing features of the Internet exist in Open Content, Creative Commons[1] and Web 2.0, the second stage of the Internet is leading to a consolidation of a an open, global Internet culture.

Realisation of this kind of thinking and operational practice requires a deep cultural change in the information awareness of people, business operation methods, the information culture of organisations and an extension of information awareness to the furthest limits of society. Understanding of the procedures and effects of transparent Internet culture and the implementation of new possibilities in operations is all part of Corporate Literacy.

## Destination: a literate organisation

Comprehensive Literacy of companies is nowadays typically *dispersed* across the company. It is not recognised, it is poorly utilised and the connection with company strategy is missing. Financial Literacy is required, not only in the areas of financial management and administration, but throughout the business as a whole. Customer Literacy is needed for sales and marketing. Business Intelligence may take care of Information Literacy – if the unit and professionals exist within the organisation – relating to the operational environment. Media Literacy is required by the communication units, possibly complemented with Visual Literacy. The latter also links to product development and design. Research and Science Literacy is required by development and research units. Environmental Literacy is required by those parties responsible for environmental issues. The company may have spread its tentacles far and wide, but how are the signals received passed on to the parties where they are really needed and what is the reaction to these signals? In addition, how are observations made in different areas combined into a larger picture? Attentiveness has been lost and there is no foundation for focusing it throughout company as a whole. In some companies the operational environment is being studied systematically, unit by unit, and there is an effort to control information and knowledge via technical systems. However, comprehensive understanding for the utilisation of information is insufficient as regards skills and resources and there are no tools to develop it. The question to ask now is: What level of Corporate Literacy does our company have?'

Adoption and internalisation of the Corporate Literacy concept as an integral part of the company strategy, operation and development opens up new ways to identify and utilise external and internal information and knowledge and how to react to it. Corporate Literacy means the identification of strategic information areas and the creation of a *horizontal perspective* in the information environment. On the other hand, Corporate Literacy *vertically* condenses the information and communication *process* into a chain from search, recognition, browsing, obtainment, assessment, analysis and interpretation to use of the information, to the formation of new information, production and further distribution.

Corporate Literacy requires the company to have its own *information strategy*. The company has to analyse what information is important to it. Corporate Literacy means the identification, detection and focusing of the senses and tentacles of the company in accordance with this information strategy. The senses are found in human beings, networks, systems and structures that channel the information flows of the company. Different senses may have a different kind of a strategic weighting value.

Corporate Literacy is the *attitude* of the organisation as regards information and knowledge. It is a *set of mental habits* based on which good *information practices* are formed. It means active and attentive observation and a critical evaluation of information. We are talking about the corporate down-top approach that is *present* everywhere within the organisation. The process, attitude, set of mental habits and presence in all organisations are the same features that Paul Argenti and Janis Forman (2002) list in their book as the features of Corporate Communication. Corporate Literacy means that all the personnel work together leading to *empowerment* and *sharing*.

The business world should take Corporate Literacy seriously. Adoption of this approach in anticipation of the future consolidates the company from the inside, helps it to predict external changes and to react to them in time. Corporate Literacy means continuously developing skills to utilise the network information and information flows beneath the borders of the organisation. We are not talking about huge investments but mostly it means fully utilising the investments already made in the development of the company personnel, information technology and the expertise of the staff and in the possibilities created by information networks. Corporate Literacy also leads to the ability to assess the shortages in information systems and channels and how to correct them.

Corporate Literacy will lead to savings in costs. The bigger the effort made to develop Corporate Literacy, the clearer the understanding within the whole of the organisation about what information is important and what kind of information is obtained, monitored and organised for investment. Corporate Literacy will also lead to more effective information practices and, simultaneously, to more effective information searches, attainment, processing and production processes. These matters are important but, of even greater importance are than the savings in costs, are the new possibilities and the understanding that Corporate Literacy opens up within an organisation.

# Note

1. The Creative Commons (CC) is a non-profit organisation devoted to expanding the range of creative work available to others legally to build upon and share. The Creative Commons website enables copyright holders to grant some of their rights to the public while retaining others through a variety of licensing and contract schemes. The intention is to avoid the problems current copyright laws create for the sharing of information. http://en.wikipedia.org/wiki/Creative_Commons (accessed 2 February 2006)

# 3

# Information skills and roles

People structure the senses of an organisation, founded on the complementary and consolidating literacy of the people working in the organisation. Work and all daily activities require multifield information and Media Literacy, the ability to assess information critically as provided by the Internet, media and other information sources and resources as well as the courage to participate and express themselves via network communication methods. If we do not develop our literacy, we will become involuntary jack-in-the-boxes controlled by information and media flows. If our consciousness passively fills with the messages pushed at us, our ability to think and act independently will wither and our ability to make decisions will weaken. Multifield Literacy is a part of global citizenship and citizen skills, which should be taught at primary school level. It is not just a survival skill but also a mental self-defence skill.

It is obvious that professionalism includes the ability to analyse the current situation and past events, to predict the future, to obtain, assess and distribute information independently as well as in a social working environment. In addition to these skills, the diffusion of professionalism requires a positive attitude and procedures encouraging and supporting the formation of shared information. It is important for everyone to understand their own informational roles and responsibilities: their individual contribution to the formation of shared information. Everyone is responsible within their own understanding at least, for their field of influence in their close surroundings and the information and communication produced and used within it. We cannot manage alone but with our different skills and knowledge, we can support each other.

# Users as producers: information skills needed by everyone

The production and publication of information was previously the monopoly of only a few experts. The distribution of information took place as though it constituted the commands of an omnipotent dictator, issuing directives from on high, to the grateful and obedient masses. Universities, prestigious private publishers, as well as national and international authorities produced information. The roles of information producers and users remained separate. We are now closer to a situation where almost everyone functions dually as a user and producer of information both at work and in all other facets of daily existence. This weakens the position of institutions and authorities and breaks down the power structure of information. The long prevailing arrangement according to which some are information producers and others information users does not hold anymore.

Information skills needed by everyone cover the information and Media Literacy chain from attainment, search and critical assessment of information in different forms, to personal production, communication and influence of information in the digital information and media environment. Everyone needs practical skills in addition to technical skills in order to plan their own activities and to apply their expertise via different connections and equipment. Awareness about personal rights and possibilities to influence are part of multifield literacy. Not everyone needs to know and do everything; the skills and knowledge of people complement each other. What is essential is that people are recognised and respected as participants who are able to critically assess information and actively construct shared understanding and knowledge. Everyone has something to give, and this simple fact should constitute a prominent factor in the practical consideration surrounding the construction of information environments and their contents.

The use of the Internet, in and of itself, develops the informational skills of individuals in previously unimaginable ways. The use of Internet search engines, web page browsing and email communication are activities, which inevitably, stimulate independent thought and communication via tools and within an environment over which the individuals themselves can exert personal control. Already, research results relating to Internet use contradict the notion that Internet separates people from each other, but rather indicate that communality is developing across the Internet, which at its best can promote a more inclusive and empathic approach to information and communication behaviour. Based on the studies in the PEW/Internet project, 60 million Americans have turned to the Internet for help in making major life decisions. The Internet helps to maintain people's social networks, and provides connectivity to members of their social network in times of need, even crisis (Horrigan et al. 2006). When researching the construction of games by young people have indicated the importance they place on leaving their own tracks across the Internet as evidence of their participation and influence.

The social bookmarking or folksonomy phenomenon created in Internet guides facilitate via bookmarks, graphics, key words or tags, the leaving of traceable footprints to attract like-minded individuals. Providing meta-information[1] has become a communal action. It should be expanded to become a part of common informational behaviour throughout all existing information systems and net services. Providing meta-information should be as self-evident as applying a title to an article or giving a name to a publication.

With the world shrinking and networking, the dependency of people on each other increases. Therefore, procedures supporting information distribution and communality become informational skills required by everyone. The burden of information searching across the net environment has been transferred to the users of information. All of the information providers carry the responsibility for accessibility, ensuring the obstacles to accessibility are surmountable. As the user of information is increasingly also the producer of information, s/he better understands this responsibility. However, an ever increasing emphasis on individual skills and knowledge is untenable. The only realistic option is to strengthen communal literacy where the skills of different people complement each other and everyone is supported by the total literacy of an organisation.

## Literacy skills as a part of professional skills and expertise

In an organisation, each employer should have:

- an ability to outline and recognise the information environment and its information sources;

- skills to use the information sources and information systems common to the organisation and related to their own work;

- skills to use the information sources of the open net and information media;

- skills relating to information production including, in addition to the core content, the production of meta-information

- skills of cooperation, as well as communication and networking skills;

- knowledge of the most important principles of the legislation and concomitant ethical procedures connected with the use of information.

I have been involved in the education and training with the terms of the personnel within Finnish ministries with the goal of strengthening this form of content of Information Literacy. The training programmes have followed the kind of themes mentioned above and have proved themselves effective. It is particularly effective to carry out the training within the actual working environment as this promotes communal learning and facilitates a sharing of knowledge, networking and cooperation between participants in both the short and the long term.

The delineation of an information environment within an organisation should constitute a key part of the initial training given to every new employee. The delineation of one's own information environment opens one's eyes to new horizons. It enables the identification of diverse and versatile information sources in use, from information systems and network service to organisational sources and experts, from statistics to studies, from numeral and text formats to audiovisual information. If people do not outline their information environment comprehensively, they are obliged to rely routinely upon a narrow range of familiar information sources. In practice, they are blinkered to many fresh possibilities and novel information flows. Then the information structures become frozen in both time and place. The ability to delineate the information environment of a company, a community or one's own personal information space, identifying both possibilities and limitations, is an essential skill to which everyone requires access and is a crucial aspect of Corporate Literacy.

Delineating the Internet environment with its search engines, directories and other information tools is an important aspect of the knowledge relating to the current information environment. Understanding the characteristics and differences of the structures, search engines and directives relating to Internet information contents, the formation of information search strategy and the ability to critically assess search results, constitute skills that need to be inculcated in experts, managers and all administrative and general personnel at all levels. The majority of people currently using the Internet are familiar with Google but are blinkered to many other useful net tools, let alone being aware of the systematic planning underlying an information search.

Following the delineation of an information environment, it is prudent to carry out an analysis of the level of knowledge and user skills regarding the information systems and relative both to those shared within the organisation and those specific to an individual's own work. Experience tells us that there is a plethora of shortages in the workplace in terms of personal control over one's own working tools. Within an organisation everybody should know what information is available and where and which factors have an effect on whether that information can or cannot be located.

The production of information skills fully encompasses skills relating to the production of both the core content and meta-information. It is important that everyone engaged in writing documents realises that in addition to core content the need for descriptive information is ubiquitous: a title, key words, copyright and publisher information, publication dates, possibly a summary, etc. Based on these facts the information content can be located, distributed, and if deemed appropriate it can be linked to other apposite information materials. The provision of meta-information requires an empathic approach to the needs of other information users, as well as the words and phrases they are likely to employ their search for information.

The production of information within an organisation is mostly writing for the net. Increasingly the entire personnel have to be able to report, guide, prepare instructions, train and communicate effectively via the Internet. Writing for the net requires in-depth training, for example, in order to obtain *bona fide* support for work processes from the intranet. The net texts should be clear, concise items, more in accordance with the language of the readers than the jargon of the organisation. The links should facilitate straightforward reading and access to further information if required. The headline titling, link and text monikers should be informative, unambiguous and as consistent as possible so that they also work individually, while signposting a deeper route into the text. Those writing for the web need to know the structures of the linked web environment and understand the ways that people use and read web pages.

Cooperation, communication and networking skills are social skills, which are also required for the attainment, distribution and formation of information. It appears that the more we work with machines the more we have contact with people. We need to understand people well and we need clear rules for the game. The use and production of information and communication are activities that impinge upon wide-ranging issues, for example, legislation relating to copyrights, data protection, privacy, publicising of information and free speech of which it is important to have at least a working knowledge. A literate organisation obeys laws, takes care of data protection, functions ethically and respects people.

# New roles and tasks for information professionals

Corporate Literacy consists of people's individual skills complementing one other. What then, is the role of information professionals? What is required from them? Information professionals have many possible roles as promoters, supporters and experts of Corporate Literacy.

Viewing information as a part of work, information work thereby keeps pace with the changes that inevitably take place over the course of the history of work. In the case of artisans, work can be described as being linked to tacit information that could be transferred from the master to the apprentice in the immediate workplace via the novice copying the master. This dispenses with the role of the information professional as the transfer of information functions via direct communication during the act of working. Information specialisation was created along with specified divisions of work and the portioning of work relating to batch production. Planning and execution are separated from one another. The role of information professionals in an industrial society is linked to the attainment, search, saving, editing and transfer of information. The last 20 years constitute a period of improvement in processes and mass tailoring, where the task of the information specialists in a company has been to support the processes with information and create informative resources for mass tailoring. In the public sector, the work of information specialists has correspondingly been to provide support for preparation, planning, research and decision-making. The more public sector work is also viewed as processes, the more the work of information specialists can be directed to support those processes.

Victor and Boynton (1998) identify the latest historical form of work to be joint development requiring dialogic information. Both the production environment and the products are becoming increasingly complex. There are an increasing number of demanding, complex service and product entities characterised by a long life cycle and the participation of many parties in the production process. These kinds of entities include, for example, comprehensive information systems, environment protection projects and the care of the elderly. It is impossible to construct these kinds of entities through an approach based on tightly apportioned project work, as the object of work is both ambiguous and in a state of constant flux. Comprehensive, lateral dialogue is essential for the development of these kinds of service and research entities where the actual customers are involved and their needs are clearly visible.

This kind of joint development requires open communal and cooperative methods for application in the tracking, attainment, interpretation and implementation of information. Organisational limits have to be by-passed. Requirements include readily available resources and an unbiased attitude toward multiprofessional cooperation based on negotiations, in which the customer, that is, the party requiring the information acquires a strong role. If the process exhibits hasty, improvised meetings between separate parties for the solution of a shared problem or tasks, resources for the formation of flexible information specific to each task will be required.

The work of information specialists is targeting effective organisation toward a new type of task-oriented entities. The new tasks in the complex information environment no longer exhibit the previous degree of permanence; this is true for example, in the professions teacher, journalist, librarian and researcher. The contents of the tasks mentioned above still prevail but in different types of combinations. The roles and professions of information specialists are changing, overlapping and integrating with one another. When I myself have been training different kinds of information specialists, information designers and web producers, for example, the backgrounds and experience of the participants has varied from information technology to communications, document administration, information services, technical writing and business knowledge. Participants have included social scientists, lawyers, physicists, engineers, librarians, information system designers, urban planners, journalists, etc.

In multifield information work, interaction between different specialists, linking different types of information, leads to the formation of new knowledge. Technology, content and communication are interrelated in many different ways.

The role of information specialists has changed due to the possibilities provided by information networks and the development of individual and Corporate Literacy, for example, in the following ways:

- Via the Internet, the information resources are available to everyone. People search independently for information across the net environment. This moves the emphasis of the work of information specialists and librarians from information search services to the design of information architecture. The network services require planning so that information can be located. The implementation of transparent search and retrieval requires knowledge of all-round informational planning.

- The information resources and the services have to be unobstructed and accessible. Further investment is required whether one is talking of the user needs of the company director, the political decision-maker, the active citizen or the immigrant in the new environment.

- The change in the concept of learning in general, and e-learning in particular needs to an enhancement in the support of independent learning. This moves the emphasis in the work of a teacher to planning of the learning environment and implementing learning tools, thereby facilitating learning.

- The purchasing of information and the signing of agreements with international publishers and suppliers has become increasingly demanding and requires expertise in business, technology and jurisprudence.

- Organisations have to be able to assess, browse and analyse essential information and to predict matters for the support of decision-making. Tracking of multifield matters is required; interpreters and analysts are needed

- The ongoing expansion of the concepts of information and the complexity of information: data, information, knowledge, the combining of explicit and tacit information and the increasing complexity, multisemiotics and multimodality of network information affects all aspects of information work. Corporate Literacy means an ability to combine and utilise essential information based on the need and situation irrespective of its form.

Corporate Literacy requires a well-planned infrastructure and information architecture underlying the organisation.

It forms the basis and facility for the structure and formation of knowledge and opens the channels for information flows. It makes sense to build many of the services connected with information search, attainment, transmission and editing into Internet services to support independent work of the individual personnel. The knowledge of information specialists is an urgent requirement for the design and implementation of these Internet services. Information services increasingly involve the design of knowledge, learning facilities, structures and accessibility.

Previously the information services and information specialists concentrated on the search for, and attainment of, information. However, in the near future the emphasis of the tasks supporting Corporate Literacy will be on the planning of information facilities, structures and channels and for an improvement in the quality of information.

## From information attainers and suppliers to designers and builders of information facilities

The new roles and tasks include information architects, information delineators and classifiers, information designers and meta-data planners, as well as meta-data specialists.

Web-designers, librarians, programmers, information specialists and system planners have a vested interested in information architecture. The development of a new kind of information architecture is dependent upon their skills, but yet there is no definitive, detailed explication of the experiential background required of an aspiring information architect.

Information professionals have to develop design skills by familiarising themselves with approaches and methods to design and the problems design poses. It is the same as with the training of crafts people where the aim is to strengthen their independent and creative approach so that they do not simply rely on traditions through exclusive use of old patterns and modes of production. This new kind of information architecture requires courage and comprehensive vision and the ability simultaneously to consider many factors. To be able to envisage the information environment requires a 'bird's eye' view. Information content professionals have to apply their knowledge across and throughout the total concept.

The role of the Information specialist incorporates tasks more commonly associated with the professions of designer and builder in relation to the planning of information spaces and facilities, for example, is seen in Table 3.1.

**Table 3.1** Tasks of the information specialist in the planning of information spaces and facilities

| Design | Building |
| --- | --- |
| content design | information content, meta-layer |
| construction design | delineating |
| information design | processes |
| meta-data design | organisation |
| location information design | editing |
| usability design | directories |
| information architecture | glossaries, taxonomy, ontology |
| | classification |
| | description |
| | search characteristics and tools |
| | hypertext, navigation, links |

## From an indexer to meta-writers

Description of materials and indexing has traditionally been invisible work undertaken by librarians and information specialists. Now this invisible layer, giving information about information, is expanding in information networks. Network

125

information has to be delineated, classified and described in many ways to ensure its accessibility. Good quality classifications, menus and groupings are required for the outlining of contents and the outlining work itself requires knowledge and resources. Abundant description is essential and the description and search of contents requires high-quality glossaries and directories. Shared accurate concept systems – ontologies – are required for the support of the semantic web. New methods and meta-information presentations are to be developed. Knowledge and compliance of meta-information standards is by itself a separate expertise area.

Knowledge is required for this invisible meta-writing, i.e. production of meta-information and also expertise in implementation of the standards of practice. All document producers have to have basic knowledge of meta-writing in order to assign the appropriate words, write summaries and when needed, structure documents in ways allowing parts to be removed for different purposes. All the writers need knowledge of titling and labelling. Meta-information officials and meta-information experts are needed to design comprehensive systems, for the training, consultation and development of meta-information tools and methods.

## From supplier to analysts

There is an abundance of information available, and searching for it is seemingly easy. The search engines are increasingly more effective but the search results vary in their quality. There is a requirement for information assessment, interpretation and analysis. By undertaking these tasks, information professionals can justify their existence and bring added value to search engines.

Information analysts are important for the support of decision-making as well as the study and prediction of various phenomena. Information analysts should be able to connect information in different forms from different fields and to use different information research methods. They have to be skilled in interpretation and assessment of both quantitative and qualitative information. They have to adopt approaches similar to anthropology. They have to be able to connect, compare and interpret written research information, data and fieldwork observations as well as visual and audio materials.

There has always been a need for analysis but the demand for rapid reaction and response, as well as the associated need for rapid and predictive analyses has increased in financial, environmental and political matters. The work of a broad-based information analyst requires the identification of appropriate analysis and research methods from different fields and the implementation of these in business and public sector decision-making.

Information analysts also need to be able to support experts. An analysis process may include physical or virtual discussions by experts in the building of a shared analysis from which the information base of all the experts involved will benefit. Analysis and prediction networks require a global reach. Based on skilful networking and high-quality communication these can, if desired, be adopted fairly rapidly.

It is important that information professionals invest in information presentation methods, condensing, crystallising and editing information to accessible formats. User-friendliness depends upon the editing of information into a form suitable to the end-user. Paying attention to this stage is critical, irrespective of whether those needing information are company directors, political decision-makers or illiterate women in poor countries. In addition to accessibility of information suitable for the situation, coherent presentation also requires serious attention.

## From material suppliers to skilled buyers and agreement negotiators

Information is also crucial on the trading floor and has its price whether it is in printed or electronic form. One of the important roles of information specialists supported by Corporate Literacy is the purchasing of appropriate information that meets the needs of the organisation. Professional buyers with an awareness of quality and cost, not to mention strong contacts with producers, publishers, suppliers as well as the structures and operations of information industry and trading, are in big demand. They have to be able to negotiate, draft agreements and put together consortiums. They must also be aware of the contrast in quality and price determined by the variety of formats (text, visual, audio, printed, electronic, etc.) now available for the transmission of information.

## Consolidators of the senses of the organisation

If Corporate Literacy is only based on the skills of information professionals, the danger is that the information and knowledge systems will start living a life of their own, well marshalled, but free from control in terms of the results they produce. Development of information systems should not be technology-oriented, nor based solely from the perspective of information specialists. If systems are developed in this way, control and organisation of information may be of a high quality, but the usability of the systems will be weak and the information contained within them will offer little in the way of practical utilisation. The task of information professionals is to strengthen the senses of the organisation. They have to acquaint themselves thoroughly with the work undertaken throughout the organisation. They have to develop in the organisation a shared information language. One can do this via interviews, project involvement and close observation of various work groups. It would be highly beneficial if information professionals, from time to time, could work in various core tasks of the organisation, such as marketing, product development or customer service, for example. Furthermore, those working in core tasks need to undergo information training in tandem with the pursuit of informational expertise within their own field. Otherwise, information professionals may become a group that is narrowly specialised in information administration and removed from actual operations. The danger then would be that the question of what information is important and why it is important could be side-stepped.

# Note

1. Meta information is 'information about information'. Meta information can describe, for example the document conent, structure or language. It can give information about the document producer, publisher, publication date, saving format and user rights. Increasingly more information is required for finding and joining information and for assessment of content.

# 4

# Managing and leading Corporate Literacy

The creation of Corporate Literacy is a management issue. It is possible to review it from three perspectives:

- Communal literacy requires management. It is not a ready-made acquisition but rather requires determined, enthusiastic and supportive management for its targeting and development.

- Communal literacy is an additional management tool. It supports the set strategy and achievement of targets in a complex operational environment.

- The creation of Corporate Literacy requires a new kind of management approach. This starts from a reassessment of the concept of organisation and information. It is a new management area. It requires *literate* management.

Management of Corporate Literacy involves the targeting of strategic attention toward what information is important and what information is emerging. The management will create a vision of the aim and a strategy about how to proceed, including which matters are to be given emphasis or priority. Corporate Literacy requires high-level awareness about the macro-picture. In order to achieve this, the targets must be clear to all those working within the organisation. It is also important that they are all aware of the significance of their own role and their responsibility. For people to give their skills to shared use and to share their knowledge, they need positive encouragement and recognition of their contribution. This encouragement and positive attention is the task of the management.

Broadly speaking, management of Corporate Literacy means managing the matters that were dealt with in Chapter 2 (Corporate Literacy in practice), i.e. attention to what information is important, the creation of channels and structures as a base for the requirements and development of operational methods encouraging the creation of an information culture

## Corporate Literacy as an additional tool for management

Corporate Literacy is an additional management tool. The structuring of Corporate Literacy is a continuous process in the support of the strategy of an organisation or community and for the achievement of set targets. Corporate Literacy is also the basis of the formation of strategy. The better the management is able to observe, predict, analyse and interpret its operational environment, the markets' and its own functional facilities, financial and social changes, the more solid base it also has for the creation of its own strategy. Developing Corporate Literacy promotes innovative solutions, new ways of functioning, new kinds of services and products based on information. The ability to read users and customers leads to a better understanding of these needs and consequently to the development of products and services based on these needs. A literate organisation is able to read a variety of different information sources and to use different information channels and networks that improve its position and operational possibilities in our insecure, complex, global environment.

## New kind of management method

To achieve Corporate Literacy one requires a new kind of management method. The backdrop to this is the new concept of an organisation and of information, which is where we started from at the beginning of this book.

The manager of Corporate Literacy encourages a versatile use of the senses of an organisation and meets the requirements needed for it. We are talking about a reforming management method: diversity of information structures and information flows is assessed and reformed. The various parties are listened to from different angles and across the board. Conflicting and radical information is not to be rejected, but is instead actively monitored thus avoiding automatic reinforcement of current prevailing views.

The manager of Corporate Literacy is like an anthropologist observing and analysing the organisation in question using versatile methods: interviews, debates, by reading reports and documents. S/he manages the organisation using the language of information by anchoring via versatile information to the reality and open to new information flows.

## To Knowledge Community animators, developers and managers

Information work is undertaken producing new information increasingly emerging in the form of networks, dialogic joint development and different information communities.

The management of Corporate Literacy may also offer new roles to information professionals. This kind of work requires mobilisers, enthusiasts, developers and leaders. Management relating to people, information resources and technology, as well as leadership relating to networks and self-guiding communities is required.

The manager has to have a long-term vision and be capable of strategic and financial thinking. It may be necessary to operate within restricted resources or, if necessary, obtain further resources. Many information specialists tend to gear themselves more to the direction of the roles of experts rather than managers. In order to emphasise information more strongly by the management, it is important that information professionals gain skills useful in the carrying out of management tasks. They should not be afraid to take a stand as citizens, to express their opinion, as well as offer interpretation and conclusions based on their own expertise. Instead of wanting recognition from management, they should bring their own substance – information – to the forefront, discuss directly with the management and, if needed, to be ready to step into management.

At the beginning of the 1980s I was working as a researcher in the city culture project of the Council of Cultural Co-Operation for the Council of Europe. It involved 12 cities and the aim was encouragement and stimulation of their cultural activities from the perspective of the local population. The main topic of the project could be framed as the following: Your town, your life, your future. Many of the cities participating in the project were the so-called new towns, modern suburbs built around the capital or some other large city. They were just starting to develop their own culture. I learned a lot via this project, particularly due to my experiences of the projects of the different cities. Among the wide-ranging and rich cultural activities being held, the so-called animators (French: animateur) found centre stage, enthusing, encouraging, maintaining and supporting the activities of the local population in many ways. The managers of the local projects and innovations should also occupy an equivalent role.

Communities forming information require versatile managers as developers of their literacy. Here is another role that information professionals should also train for and it is a role they should, when needed, take into their working environment.

## Creating circumstances for a Knowledge Garden

An old garden can surprise you if you do not control it strictly and restrict the growth of its plants. Occasionally the earth reveals plants whose seeds have been lying dormant beneath earth for hundreds of years. They will prosper if their growing conditions improve and one is able to expose them to sunshine and provide space enough to grow. If the maintenance of the garden operates along strict lines of planning oblivious to unimagined possibilities, then surprises such as dormant seeds springing into bloom are impossible.

Similar options exist within the management of an organisation and its literacy. Management can provide space for self-guiding growth and development or alternatively, the organisation operates along strictly controlled lines that do not allow for any new growth. Most of the organisations – both in the private and public sector – need a strategic vision, a utilisation of the senses, a reformation of the structures of information and communication, an opening of new information channels, and innovative and creative solutions in our rapidly changing, uncertain global environment. Management based on Corporate Literacy creates prosperous conditions for the garden of knowledge.

# 5

# Corporate Literacy in different contexts

The development of Corporate Literacy can take place in any organisation or community irrespective of whether it exists on an international, global or local scale, or whether it represents the private or public sectors. In this chapter I will be exploring Corporate Literacy from three different aspects: Corporate Literacy in a company, Corporate Literacy in a government and local collaborative Literacy.

## Corporate Literacy in a company

The building of Corporate Literacy depends upon targets, personnel, the corporate image, the corporate networks and the corporate culture. Therefore, the process of becoming literate is unique to each company.

In business, information and knowledge have no intrinsic value. The value of information is in the fact that it supports business activities. However, very few companies have carefully identified and analysed which information areas are of key importance to the company. This is not to say that, in recent decades at least, the companies have not invested plenty of capital while paying attention to information technology and the administration information and knowledge. What *has* been lacking is the paying of attention to the actual information and knowledge rather than simply the generation and management of them. We need this approach now, but it will not be easy. Via information technology, various forms of information have been 'found' from stage to stage and technologies have been developed to administer these: information management, Knowledge Management, data warehouse, document management and content management. It is a lot easier to talk about different forms of information and administration of these forms than information itself.

However, when the form of information can more or less be controlled and sequestered, it is time to take our collective heads out of the clouds. Nowadays, hardly anyone questions the role of information as a part of business operations. Therefore, companies have to build their own information and knowledge strategies. They have to take a stand on the Really Big Questions: What kind of information do they really need? What information is of key importance to them? This involves inspection of lateral information areas, the building of one's own information map, and the identification of multiform information sources. Information strategy also means taking a stand on which information areas need 'fast' information, weak predicting signals as regards changes and on which areas show development processes should be followed. The past, present and the future have to be monitored and analysed simultaneously.

Corporate Literacy requires a thorough understanding of the customers needs, evident in the products and services under development, throughout the company as a whole. Corporate Literacy means that the company has a good understanding of the society and the culture it operates within, of people's expectations and of the effects of one's own operations across and within the environment. A company operating globally requires a deep understanding of different cultures, religions and political and religious value judgements, or at the very least needs to be making conscious effort to achieve such an understanding. The management of a literate company also knows its staff, their skills and views, supports staff development and values the views of staff members. Corporate Literacy extends throughout all levels of the company and the whole organisation is aware of the shared targets and the operational principles.

The company builds up this multilevel literacy by identifying its own senses and by strengthening them. They help it to sound its passage forward in the uncertain and changing environment. The company has to develop ways to arrange and organise information, to create and renew structures and space that is open to new information flows. Corporate Literacy maintains not only upon its own structures and channels, but also, upon information space and information flows expanding the networks, as well as partners and interest groups of the company. Company management has to have a shared understanding relating to this entity. It all starts from the point at which the company takes responsibility for the management of Corporate Literacy thus developing its own literacy and its own process along the way to becoming literate.

In the development of Corporate Literacy, the key personnel are the information and communications specialists of the company whose roles and tasks have to be modernised in response to the rapidly changing demands of the information environment. An organisation developing its own literacy needs the expertise of information designers, information architects, information analysts, usability designers, meta-data experts, facilitators, etc. Work by information specialists, knowledge and communication is integrated to be a part of the processes and business activities by companies.

Corporate Literacy does not necessarily usher in a new dawn. It only means that the matters are being investigated with fresh pairs of eyes. Corporate Literacy means that information structures and channels are simultaneously undergoing a constant process of assessment and renewal so that the company, like a snake sheds and renews its own skin.

# Corporate Literacy in government

The task of government is that of solving international, national, regional and local problems, while planning ahead and predicting the possible effects of decisions, which have and will be taken. These tasks include the effective and efficient organisation of health, educational, social and infrastructural services for the citizens.

Globalisation requires literacy relating to different regions and cultures even more widely than ever before. Governmental units often operate in metropolises and therefore need to pay special attention in understanding the contrasting living-conditions and competing problems and concerns of people living within a spectrum that has wealth and poverty at its extremes. People, companies and jobs move from country to country and fundamentally change the economic, social and cultural structure of the areas they move to, and indeed, from. The effects between areas are not limited to a single town, state or continent but are extremely complex and can suddenly cast a surprisingly wide net.

In order to perform its tasks well, the government requires a solid, current, regularly updated knowledge base. Government has to have access to the latest information from as wide a range of sources as possible. The government should be able to sieve the essential information, interpret and to apply it in its decision-making. New issues need tackling simultaneously and with immediacy in today's complex environment. Following rules and regulations in the manner of a bureaucratic organisation is no longer a tenable approach. New knowledge and innovation should be the order of the day.

In a communication environment where many channels and ranges of equipment are used, the authorities needs specialised skills to function as a single, united body, which is capable of responding rapidly and flexibly across the net. Administration requires broad-based Corporate Literacy for monitoring what is going on and sensitive antennae for the reception of signals from different channels and sources. Correct information does not move with institutions and their hierarchies. Critical literacy and new methods for rapid assessment of the reliability of information are required.

When considering the current tasks it is important to ask how the government currently reads its environment. What is the information upon which decisions are prepared and made?

Government needs multifield literacy. For the implementation of democracy, it is important to know who has the ear of the government. Are the unemployed being listened to on matters relating to employment? Are old people being listened to on matters relating to their care? Are small businesses being listened to when discussing the development of new areas? Are researchers being listened to on environmental matters? It is extremely important to pay attention to information structures and channels via which the government reads or listens to citizens, their organisations, commerce, trade and the results of scientific research. The government needs to be able to predict the future while taking action where previous decisions are having an adverse effect in the present. The government also has to have an understanding of history; what have been the effects of decisions made in the past. Literacy of both small processes and unexpected phenomena is an ongoing requirement in the promotion of good, responsible government.

It is important to analyse the actual methods for the exploitation of information sources as the information environment has changed in such a revolutionary manner. Previously, a colleague was perhaps the first port of call in the pursuit of information. Nowadays, it could well be google.com instead. Easy access to superficial surface information is misleading. Information search skills, an understanding of Internet structures and the critical evaluation of information requires a lot of training throughout the whole of society, including civil servants and decision-makers.

The influence of the media as regards the formation of information is significant. Messages fly back and forth 24 hours a day in public transport, in shops, on the streets and at home. Those working for the government are as vulnerable to commercial communication as other citizens. The media and brands integrate into new information, news and even research. Facts and fiction become mixed. The ethical restrictions of journalism have been fading as regards commercial communication. Sound bites are on the increase and this type of news language is often ambiguous with references to resources are less than clearly stated. Those working for the government should be highly skilled – LITERATE – in their ability to read the media and to interpret critically commercial, political and other hidden messages.

Government needs an information strategy that defines and makes visible the information areas and sources important to the preparation of policies, decision-making and service activities that require active monitoring. Great challenges relating to governmental literacy include the combining of various fields and an understanding of the theatres of influence. The formation of literacy in government is possible only through the literacy of governmental officials and its supporting processes. The key task for information specialists working in government is to awaken awareness about the need to develop information and Media Literacy and actively assess and promote the versatility of information sources and their use. In the easily accessible surface information world, the information specialists have to signpost the versatility of the information environment, increase the visibility openness, vertical depth and lateral direction of the information channels to encompass different areas, conflicting sources and the past, present and the future.

## Access to usable information: empowerment of people

In a democratic society, preparation and decision-making relating to the issues at hand should be transparent. Both the realisation of citizens' rights and accountability require that access to information is freely available. Information networks and e-government enable the transparency of the decision-making processes, the availability of documents and the possibility for citizens to influence the issues before they are set in stone. In an open society, the government has to actively share information, promote openness and good practice concerning information. Public information is common capital and a resource for all.

Government needs user-oriented information design. Legal information is an example of essential social information material, which in almost all parts of the world is difficult for citizens to access. In many countries, the laws are not available to the public via Internet. Even in the countries where all of the legislation is available in the net, legal information can be difficult to find and understand. Citizens need juridical literacy, knowledge of legislative terminology and legal structures. Government should try to remove the structural obstructions that prevent the finding and an understanding of legal information.

Legal information, technically, can be easily posted on the Internet so that it is accessible to everyone. This is a new situation for legislators to find themselves in. If the information architecture is designed from the point of the user, it will ease the connection of legal information to other matters in various network services. Then the citizens will be able to get direct information relating to their rights, responsibilities, laws and their background without always needing to consult some professional party (see Horrigan et al. 2006). It should be a priority in the writing of a legal text so that the citizens can understand it. Then also members of the parliament who make decisions on laws will be able to understand it better. In order for people to follow the preparation of new laws, the stages of the legislation require a style of description that reflects ordinary people's language. This means empowerment of people. They could then independently clarify their own rights and directly use the law in the matters concerning them. The countries that are currently in the process of building their democracy have a possibility to target directly democracy of information. For countries that have formed clumsy, hierarchical structures full of governmental jargon the journey will be harder and take longer. Global citizenship should involve an expansion of the right to attain information to an international level. People and companies moving from one country to another should have access to information relating to the legislation of any country.

The question of how to get to people the information they need in acute, life-changing, decision-making situations is one facing the whole world. Government as a producer of information has a central role in all countries to place the information resources of the whole world in the forefront of assistance in the positive development of people's lives, health, financial position and the creation of balanced societies.

# Local literacy: collaborative literacy by local communities

I vividly remember a poster I saw in an underground walkway in Heathrow Airport: Don't forget local knowledge. The slogan related to various picture posters showing local traditional skills in different parts of the world. That sentence made one to stop as it was placed in a huge international airport, where the dominant trait is that of arriving and departing to and from different parts of the world. It was a striking message, particularly to those travellers who have forgotten their roots and instead identify themselves with the global transnational elite, believing that wisdom is to be found only in their individual mode of life.

It made one ponder, as to what is that local knowledge, as well as what is its meaning. How could it be connected with Corporate Literacy? In the beginning of the book I defined Corporate Literacy as the skill an organisation or community activates to 'read', observe, interpret, understand, evaluate and negotiate the context within which it operates. Collaborative literacy is a communal ability to utilise in many different ways the existing information, information networks, literature, research and expertise.

A local community can be a part of a big city, suburb, rural village or some other regional community. Regional communities may not necessarily divide in accordance with official areas nor may they have any official status. Different countries have very differently organised regional government, borders of municipalities and counties, status and regional decision-making. Local communities, just huge cities do, struggle with economic, health, social, city and urban planning, educational and cultural issues all over the world. Historical and social conditions vary greatly but the common bond is the commitment of the people living and working near each other to their living environment and to each other.

Local literacy can be viewed, for example, from the perspective of how the people deciding about regional and national matters and the experts involved working with these matters are able to read and understand the local communities and their knowledge. On the other hand, it could also be viewed from the perspective of how a local community gains information from the world outside, what is the level of its own literacy and what is the relationship between the local knowledge and the information resources of the world? An important question is how we can strengthen local literacy.

Local knowledge is often a result of the transmission of a long history and culture based upon experience and tradition. It may be that the condition necessary for survival lies within the local conditions. It can be unique. It is not always an entirely positive resource as it may be associated with local beliefs and traditions that are prohibitive to local development and cause, for example, discrimination against women or ethnic minorities. Local knowledge may uphold old beliefs, superstitions or manipulation of interests serving the interests of local power holders and thus maintaining the *status quo* at the local level.

The problems relating to informative isolation can be intolerably difficult and appear beyond any obvious solutions. I was listening in 2004 IFLA (International Federation of Library Associations) conference in Buenos Aires to a session in which the topic of debate was democracy, Information Literacy and the position of women in localised society. A young Nigerian woman was talking about the situation in her own location where the problems include AIDS, large families with many children and the fact that very few women have access to information. Eighty per cent of them are illiterate. The speaker herself was a librarian. She said that 0.4% of the Muslim women in her place of residence visit libraries and very few even know the existence of libraries. Men do not allow the women to visit libraries or create any groups of their own. Women do not know how to protect themselves against AIDS or where to go to a hospital. Men believe that a cure for AIDS is to have sexual interaction with a virgin. Contraception is never an acceptable topic for discussion. Consequently, men further spread the disease among young women. The mortality rate of women in the region is one of the highest in the world. This desperate speaker asked how libraries could distribute information to women as women do not visit libraries and are not able to meet each other. Women do not come looking for information because they do not know how to or are prevented from doing so or do not even know that this information exists. The participants had many suggestions but many of them were not, in the opinion of the speaker, functional. For example films that might otherwise be an accessible media, tend to fuel the spread of AIDS by romanticising sexual relationships while remaining silent about the dangers.

My mother who was born in the early 1900s said: 'When there is no knowledge, it is as if walking in darkness'. She was born in a poor northern country, which in the space of a mere one hundred years developed a level of national literacy and mathematical skills internationally recognised as the best in the world. She saw this poor country develop into an industrial welfare state where everyone has access to education and the majority of the population are skilled in the use of modern information equipment, libraries and the Internet. Change is possible. People need access information, in some way or another, even if they are unable to search for it. A possible solution to the problem referred to in the session in Buenos Aires, might be found via mobile technology as at least some of the women may have access to a mobile. Alternatively, it is the men who need targeting, as it is their values and beliefs that present a danger to the health of the whole community. Men with a more enlightened view need encouragement toward active involvement in trying to influence and change the views of other men. It is also possible that the children of the women or at least some of them will have access to a $100 computer and can teach their mothers to read and use the computer. Whatever the strategy for providing a given solution it is important to obtain an accurate understanding of the local situation, of possibilities open to the local population, as well as existing channels through which people can learn the skills to obtain and use information. Solutions may come from somewhere else in the world, through innovative use of technology and the adoption of local operational models, though not necessarily from industrial countries but from other equivalent regions. Collaborative literacy is required for the attainment of this knowledge. The role of the local population is itself critical.

There hardly exist any separate societies in our networked, shrunken and 'flattened' modern world, neither is anything entirely local. Therefore, not all matters can be resolved based on local knowledge. Furthermore, geographically isolated local communities are in many ways dependent in the rest of the world and the changes taking place in it. They need channels to the outside world: to research information relating to health, agriculture, environmental care, building, trading and to facilitate interaction with the rest of the world.

Local communities should be able to utilise the information resources of the world and the information sources relating to health care, environmental information, economics, jurisprudence and human rights, in particular. Equally, local knowledge needs linkage with the information resources of the world. Local societies can in many ways gain from the exchange of mutual information and modes of action. This kind of information exchange could help them to move forward in their development. This kind of joining and construction of local and global knowledge is in its early infancy.

Urban planning often fails in the challenge of recognising local needs and wishes. Urban planning in the industrial countries aims for efficiency and functionality and it has been relatively successful. The consequence has been the formation of unilateral states that have seen an erasing of the tracks of life, states where people only go to bed early in order to wake up early for work the following morning. Life has undergone a pruning of activity down to driving between work, shopping centres and housing. The inhabitants of these towns do not love the ugly shopping centres, monotonous motorways and the uninspiring suburbs that all look the same. They often love the areas that have not gone through any planning, such as the woods and shores of lakes remaining in the ever-decreasing spaces between the planned areas. They want to defend local services, such as small libraries, neighbourhood schools, the less smart local shops, children's play areas and local pubs. They want signs of life and face-to-face interaction rather than the ruthless efficiency that constitutes the ultimate goal of authoritative planning.

In his book, *The Rise of The Creative Class*, Richard Florida (2002) describes an example in his hometown, of the decision-makers wanting to build a large sports hall to attract new inhabitants. However, in reality, the so-called creative professionals whom the town officials are hoping to attract long for a vibrant, living culture, expressed through small-scale events and a diverse street life. The desire, on the part of the decision-makers, to build large, pompous-looking monuments against the wishes of the local people is also a well-known phenomenon around the world.

Often local communities are unable to find ways to exert an influence. They function between the squeeze of regional government, authorities and decision-makers. In the networked world, they have the chance to get support from each other; to exchange experiences and ideas and even to operate and have an impact working together. They could exploit in a positive way, the global methods that are currently in use by other communities, such as criminal organisations, terrorists, radical environmental movements, operating outside the official structures.

The Internet already provides the opportunity for many local communities to gain access to the information resources of the world and to communicate and cooperate with each other. From 1970 to 1980 I was employed as a researcher in the city culture project of the Council of Cultural Co-Operation of the Council of Europe where the aim was the development of city culture in 12 European cities. At that time, the only possibility for networking, meeting, exchanging research information and holding discussions between these cities was by travelling to joint meetings somewhere in Europe. Those attending the meetings were dragging home piles and piles of paper relating to information, experiences and modes of activity from the other cities. This was the case only a short time ago. Now information can virtually be shared, distributed and discussed in an entirely different way. Meetings are still a part of the overall process but networking is much more flexible and versatile. It can happen even if there are no funds for travel costs or organising a conference. All one needs is a computer, an Internet connection, skills to obtain information and the creation of contacts and operational patterns. The development of a cost-effective technology makes it easier to spread it to poor areas of the world. In addition to the provision of cheap computers, a lot of work needs to go into the creation of usability of information sources and the expansion of local literacy.

Fundamental questions at the local level:

- How do we get information to the people who need it?

- How do we create improved informational formats, which are usable by these people?

- How do we support local development work via on information?

- What do we need to do to develop local literacy?

- How do we get government, authorities and political decision-makers to understand the needs, wishes and targets of local communities and to act together with these communities rather than adopting an approach that is top down?

- How do we create a global network of villages and urban districts where the local communities can exchange and connect their operational patterns and ideas?

- How do we edit information into forms that are usable in local practice?

■ How do we encourage the adoption of already existing information so that it can be widely utilised?

## Developing local literacy

The following matters are required for the development of local literacy in the local community:

■ party/parties starting the development and party/parties taking it forward

■ operational strategy

■ identification and delineation of local knowledge

■ an information strategy on which development of literacy is based on.

The following is required in order to get information sources locally and widely utilised:

■ a responsibility on the producers of information to ensure that it can be widely utilised (the role and information responsibility of information producers)

■ the editing of information into a form that can be used and understood locally (language, culture, form, channel).

There is no way forward without people, their dreams and deeds. A local community needs initiators and promoters – active parties – of communal activities. The activities have to have targets originating from inside the community and have wide support in the community.

The community has to identify its knowledge and its own information sources and resources. It is a foundation upon which the community can build and thus move forward. There is often a lot more of this kind of knowledge and these kind of skills available than is realised. Resources include people who can purchase, edit and/or interpret information for use by the community. This kind of resource might be a local librarian, teacher, doctor, nurse or some other comprehensively literate, skilled person. Her/his task is to develop methods via which the community will get the correct information for the required purpose.

Local information strategy targets literacy toward important issues from the perspective of the community. It provides guidelines, to local libraries or schools about what information needs to be highlighted and provided for use by the community. A library is not just a public collection but it also has a local development-political task. Based on a clear strategy a community information and communication centre can be built offering the required tools for attainment and editing of information. This can be a library, or a school or some other public facility. Via WWW pages a local community can build up a network identity through which it can publicise itself and create outside contacts. In locations where Internet connectivity is already accessible to all of the local population, they can directly obtain information and communicate via the net as long as they are provided with the required training, guidance and support.

The authorities, government, researchers, companies, libraries and media as information providers are responsible for the production of information that is easily accessible, usable and connective in terms of other information. Information requires editing and structuring suitable for the net environment and needs equipping with the required meta-information. Simultaneous global and local modes of thinking and responsibility are required from an information producer as s/he has to figure out where and who are the people needing the information. Information is largely culture- and language-bound and therefore there is a lot to take into consideration when editing information for widespread use.

Awareness of an information producer as regards any obstacles in the transmission of information and factors for reducing their effect and careful information design assist in the flow of information. Open and free accessibility from the point of view is important.

Communal literacy gives the population of local communities the resources to take development into their own hands and survive independently even in difficult conditions. Local literacy reduces dependency upon central government and administrative structures. Via information networks, local communities on the periphery of society can exchange information and network with each other irrespective of where they are located. They can connect external information to their own local knowledge and obtain support to their commerce, trade, education, health care and building programmes.

This is the way to construct global information, network ecology and an informative infrastructure, which simultaneously operates on local and global terms. Information producers are required to place the global informational local communities in the particular local context. It requires thinking based on information distribution: Who else might need this information? How can one help that person access this information? The journey is long but the tools and opportunities to complete this journey do exist.

# 6

# Not seeking new lands, but seeing with new eyes

In a networked, work and operational environment overloaded with information and messages, detection of essential information, connections between matters and delineation of total concepts are difficult. The world appears complex and fragmented. The foundation for conclusions and decision-making is unreliable. Information is not *manageable*, even though specifically it is management into which, plenty of energy is invested.

Organisations are faced with complex questions, irrespective of whether they are companies, public institutions or local communities. The problem is not a lack of information. There is more information available than can actually be utilised. The search for answers and solutions is based on people, their goals and abilities in complementing each others' skills. In this book, in an attempt to provide a possible answer to these problems I have attempted to delineate the concept and development of Corporate Literacy, which initially, was defined as having skills to 'read', observe, interpret, understand, evaluate and negotiate the context within which individuals or organisations operate. The skills of individuals alone are insufficient. In the development of Comprehensive Literacy the organisations have to find their own 'senses' and utilise them for attainment of common goals.

So far we know very little about the essence of literacy: information. However, we may be getting closer all the time to understanding what information is and even how to measure it (see Baeyer 2003). Currently we are only able to measure the quantity of information based on the number of bits; at some stage in the future we may be able to undertake measurements based on the reliability, correctness and usability of information. Then it might be possible to assess more accurately the literacy skill status and the quality of information used than is currently the case.

However, Corporate Literacy is a continuously changing process rather than a static mode of operation that can be measured accurately. Our view on information as well as on organisation has expanded, become obscured and is possibly disintegrating, which means that it has to be reassembled. Networked organisations are based on human interaction, which is being continuously reshaped. The information of an organisation is formed in a process-type of way via joint construction. It needs to be supported by the process of becoming literate. It means the development of information skills and new tasks and roles relating to management via which the construction process of Corporate Literacy is supported.

The first thing is to decide what the goals are. The more insecure the environment the more important it is to be aware of one's own goals. Based on this awareness it is possible to create a strategy relating to where the attention should be directed: what information is required and what kind of information structures and channels are needed for the attainment of this information. Corporate Literacy requires a new kind of information architecture and information culture with in-built features such as visibility of information, empowerment and information and skill sharing. It requires everyone to contribute to the process. Every individual is, within the framework of his/her skills, responsible for the information produced and shared by him/her.

Corporate Literacy moves the emphasis from management to the use of information. Corporate Literacy integrates Information Management, Document Management, Knowledge Management, Content Management and technologies with the strategic goals of the organisation. The organisation learns by developing multifield literacy, to interpret and utilise in a versatile way the information and knowledge existing in various management systems, technical and human networks and information sources. An organisation learns to comprehensively utilise in many different ways, the information relating to the present situation, as well as past and possible future situations, while keeping abreast of what the external physical and network environment is offering in different forms. Corporate Literacy is directed both at current, rapidly changing information and at the slow knowledge relating to deep-lying development processes underneath.

**Figure 6.1**   Discovering the senses – finding the meaning

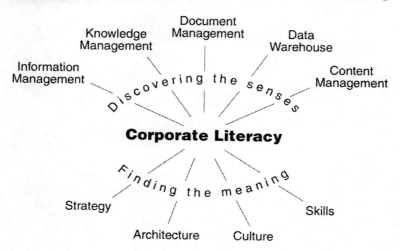

157

An anonymous Turkish woman who learnt to read as an adult, stated in a newspaper interview in 2001, 'When learning to read the eyes open and it becomes possible to see oneself and the world in a new light'. Her expression was similar to an earlier one made by Marcel Proust (1871–1922): 'The real voyage of discovery consists not in seeking new lands, but in seeing with new eyes.' By promoting universal access to information (including those lacking the economic resources), the states and the international community will be able to create new development resources for the future. Through the development of Corporate Literacy, a company, government or a local community will be able to see its existing condition and potentials with new eyes and as a consequence find new operational alternatives. Even when all the doors appear to be shut, a window may be open somewhere.

# Bibliography

American Library Association. Information Literacy Competency Standards for Higher Education. http:// www.ala.org/ala/acrl/acrlstandards/ informationliteracycompetency.htm (accessed 11 August 2005).

Argenti, P. A. and Forman, J. (2002) *The Power of Corporate Communication: Crafting the Voice and Image of Your Business*. New York: McGrawHill.

Bawden, D. and Robinson, L. (2001) Training for Information Literacy: Diverse approaches. *Online Information 2001 Proceedings*.

von Baeyer, H. C. (2004) *Information. The New Language of Science*. London: Phoenix.

Edgar, D. (2000) *Albert Speer* (a play based on Gitta Sereny's biography of Hitler's architect). London: Nic Hern Books.

Florida, R. (2002) *The Rise of the Creative Class: And How It's Transforming Work, Leisure, Community and Everyday Life*. New York: Basic Books.

Friedman, T. L. (2005) *The World is Flat: A Brief History of the Twenty-first Century*. New York: Farrar, Straus and Giroux.

Fruchter, A. and Emery, K. (1999) *Teamwork: Assessing Cross-disciplinary Learning*. Computer Support for Collaborative Learning (CSCL) 1999: December 12–15, 1999. Palo Alto, CA: Stanford University, pp. 166–173.

Helsingin Sanomat (2005) 'Interview of sea captain Kari Reinivuo', *Helsingin Sanomat*, 28 August, E5.

Horrigan, J., Boase, J., Rainie, L. and Wellman, B. (2006) Report. The Strength of Internet Ties: The internet and email aid users in maintaining their social networks and provide pathways to help when people face big decisions. http://www.pewinternet.org/PPF/r/172/report_display.asp

International Labour Office (2004) *A Fair Globalization: Creating Opportunities for All.* World Commission on the Social Dimension of Globalization. Geneva: International Labour Office.

Johansson, F. (2004) *The Medici Effect: Breakthrough Insight at the Intersection of Ideas, Concepts and Cultures.* Boston, MA: Harvard Business School.

Kauhanen-Simanainen, A. and Karivalo, M. (2002) *Corporate Literacy—Yrityksen uusi lukutaito.* Helsinki: CIM Communication & Information Management (In Finnish).

Koenig, M. E. D. (2005) KM moves beyond the organization: the opportunity for librarians. http://www.ifla.org/IV/ifla71/papers/123e-Koenig.pdf

Lewandowsky, S., Stritzke, W. G. K., Oberauer, K. and Morales, M. (2005) 'Memory for fact, fiction and misinformation. The Iraq War 2003', *Psychological Science* 16: 190–195.

Lyman, P. and Varian, H. R. (2003). How Much Information? http://www.sims.berkeley.edu/research/projects/how-much-info-2003

Meadows, D. H., Randers, J. and Meadows, D. L. (2004) *Limits to Growth: The 30-Year Update.* White River Jct, VT: Chelsea Green Publishing.

Müller, K. (2003) *Aivokutinaa.* Työterveyslaitos (Finnish Institute of Occupational Health), Helsinki.

Nardi, B. A. and O'Day, V. L. (1999) *Information Ecologies.*

*Using Technology with Heart*. Cambridge, MA: The MIT Press.

Nielsen, J. (2005) 'Enterprise Usability. Nielsen's Alertbox', November 7, 2005. http://www.useit.com/alertbox/enterprise.html

Nonaka, I. and Takeuchi H. (1995) *The Knowledge-Creating Company: How Japanese Companies Create the Dynamics of Innovation*. New York: Oxford University Press.

Orna, E. (2004) *Information Strategy in Practice*. Aldershot, Hants: Gower Publishing Limited.

Robertson, D. S. (1998) *The New Renaissance. Computers and the Next Level of Civilization*. Oxford University Press.

Stacey, R. (2001) *Complex Responsive Processes in Organizations: Learning and Knowledge creation*. London: Routledge.

Stacey, R. (2003) 'Learning as an activity of interdependent people,' *The Learning Organization* 10(6): 325–331.

Varis, T. (ed.) (2005) *Uusrenessanssiajattelu, digitaalinen osaaminen ja monikulttuurisuuteen kasvaminen*. Helsinki: OKKA-säätiö.

Varis, T. (2006) 'A short story of new literacies', in *Literacies of the Digital Age* (ed. Heinonen M.). Tampere: University of Tampere.

Victor, B. and Boynton, A. C. (1998) *Invented Here: Maximizing Your Organization's Internal Growth and Profitability*. Boston, MA: Harvard Business School.

# Index

Printed in the United States
103436LV00001B/186/A

9 781843 342618